ALBERT CAMUS

Authorised English Edition
© 2012 Edition Olms AG, Zürich

EDITION OLMS AG
Willikonerstr. 10
CH-8618 Oetwil am See / Zürich
Switzerland

Mail: info@edition-olms.com
Web: www.edition-olms.com

ISBN 978-3-283-01188-8

Translation: Joseph Laredo
Typesetting: Weiß-Freiburg GmbH – Graphik & Buchgestaltung

Original Edition
© Éditions Michel Lafon, 2009
F – 92521 Neuilly-sur-Seine Cedex

A catalogue record for this book is available from the Deutsche Bibliothek
More detailed information under
http://dnb.ddb.de

Printed in China

CATHERINE CAMUS

ALBERT CAMUS
Solitude and Solidarity

With Marcelle Mahasela

Translated by
Joseph Laredo

EDITION OLMS ZÜRICH

Contents

Introduction

And I put my hand on my heart,
where, bloodied, shimmered
the seven icy shards of your diamantine laughter.
Jacques Prévert, The Broken Mirror

Albert Camus was not a father, but he was my father. I have chosen this abstract and rather daunting form of presentation – a photograph album – in an attempt to justify retracing his life.

The undertaking is in itself illusory: a life is ever-changing, full of doubts and contradictions. A life is vital. He was life itself. A photograph freezes a fraction of a second of a life for all time, on glazed paper. And we all know that life is not simply a chronological progression: as adults, we have all experienced the sudden insouciance of childlike laughter.

A life is ever-changing and I love my father's freedom. It is not for me to reveal the truth about Camus. A writer and his writings live to the extent that they speak to others, and I respect the sensibilities of all those who have taken an interest in the man and his work.

Some have even provided illumination or confirmation. Jacqueline Lévi-Valensi, for example:
"... The myths he expounded for us, far from being sophisticated lies that betray reality, reveal profound truths about the human condition, the beauty of the world, human suffering, solitude and solidarity, about man's love of life and his sometimes desperate need of happiness."
When Jacqueline Lévi-Valensi wrote this, she was referring to the writer Camus, but in it I find my father and what he taught me. In the fourteen years I spent with him, he opened the doors that have enabled me to survive and to live. Today, as then, I find life cruel but at the same time fabulously rich and beautiful. It is thanks to him that I do.
I share this privilege – and my father – with many others. I am happy to do so. In the thirty years I have been managing his oeuvre, I have received thousands of letters from all over the world. Whatever culture or society they come from, whatever subject they broach, they all have one thing in common: a feeling of brotherly love for Camus. What I am trying to say is that Camus aroused not merely intellectual interest but something far more instinctive, universal and immediate: friendship. This was because he never cut himself off from others.

He wrote: "No one can really die in peace if he has not done all he can to help others to live." He fought, often single-handedly, against all forms of oppression. Oppression can be state-imposed and therefore easily identifiable, but it is also in the air around us: "We are suffering a reign of terror because human values have been replaced by contempt for others and the worship of efficiency, the desire for freedom by the desire for domination. It is no longer being just and generous that makes us right; it is being successful." The pursuit of success leads men to exploit others. My father was one of the others, the great majority, who each day do what they have to do with dedication and determination. Anonymously.

For these reasons, with both those who know Camus and those who do not in mind, I have braved the contradictions and difficulties, accepted the imperfections and relativities of my enterprise, and attempted, with the invaluable assistance of Marcelle Mahasela, to retrace his life... through photographs and in chronological order!

My children and grandchildren, my nephews and my great-niece did not know him. For their sake I wanted to include photographs of every kind. I wanted to rediscover his laughter, his lightness, his generosity, rediscover this warm and attentive man, who let me live. I wanted to show that Albert Camus was, as Séverine Gaspari has written, "a man among men, and one who tried to be as much a man as he could".

Catherine Camus

Like those voices which soar to the highest vaults of cathedral roofs while the obscure mass of choristers pauses to let their ardent and sexless outburst reverberate to the full, like those voices whose supplications persist, without weakening, until the very point of death, like those voices so intoxicated by mysticism as to be oblivious of the dome separating them from God, like those voices at once sustained and ecstatic, fervent and tenacious, that plaintive pride that makes sense only in the context of religious sensuality, like all those voices whose purpose is not to find but to give. That is how I imagined life.

Early Works, The Moorish House, OCI, p. 968

Genesis. 1913–1936

"Thus each artist has within himself a unique spring, which is the source of everything he is and everything he says throughout his life. [...] For myself, I know that my spring is contained in *Back and Front*, in the world of poverty and sunlight that was my home for so long [...]."

Back and Front, Preface, OCI, p. 32

"Poverty, I must say, was never a handicap for me, such were the riches the sun showered upon it."

Poverty, I must say, was never a handicap for me, such were the riches the sun showered upon it. It even illuminated my sense of rebellion. If I rebelled, I think I can honestly say, it was almost always on behalf of everyone; I wanted everyone's lives to be bathed in sunlight. I am not sure that this sort of humanity was naturally in my heart, but circumstances nurtured it. As if to correct my natural indifference, I was perched midway between gloom and radiance. Poverty prevented me from believing that all is and always has been well with the world; the sunlight taught me that what has been is not all that matters in the world. I might change my life, yes, but not the world, which was the foundation of my beliefs.

Back and Front, OCI, p. 32

"[...] he had to learn by himself, grow up by himself, grow in strength and stamina, find his own morality, his own truth, learn, in fact, to be born a man and then to then to be born again, a more difficult birth, which was to be born in the eyes of others"

The First Man, OCIV, p. 861

"In fact, no one had ever taught the child what was right and what was wrong.
[...] The only thing Jacques had been able to see and feel in a moral sense was simply the daily life of this family"

The First Man, OCIV, p. 793

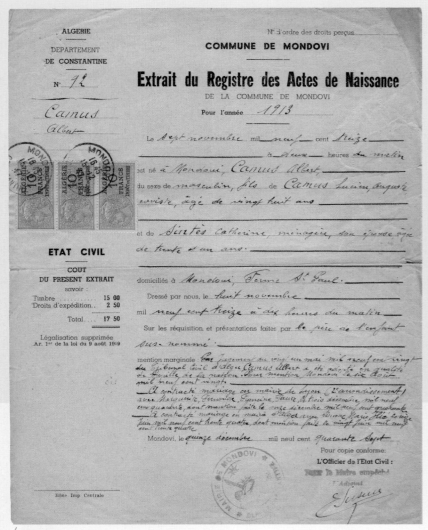

1- The Saint-Paul farm in Mondovi, Algeria, the house in which Camus was born on 7 November 1913.

2- Camus was not yet one year old when his father, who had been called up to fight with the French Zouaves, was killed in combat.

3- Camus at two.

4- Albert Camus's birth certificate.

5- Albert and his elder brother Lucien, dressed in war orphans' uniform.

6- Camus at his First Communion.

"When he walked into the workshop amid the din of the hammers, he was given a joyous welcome before the hammers continued their rhythmic dance. Ernest, wearing old, patched blue trousers, sandals coated in sawdust, a grey flannel waistcoat and a faded old fez to keep the dust and woodchips out of his handsome locks, hugged him and offered to help him."
The First Man, OCIV, p. 816

"In the end, it is only the mysteriousness of poverty that forms those with neither name nor past."

The First Man, Appendices, OCIV, p. 937

"She had a gentle and harmonious face, the curly black hair of a Spaniard, a small, straight nose and beautiful warm brown eyes."
The First Man, OCIV, p. 742

"[...] and his mother remained, just as she was, his greatest love, even though that love was tinged with despair."

The First Man, OCIV, p. 864

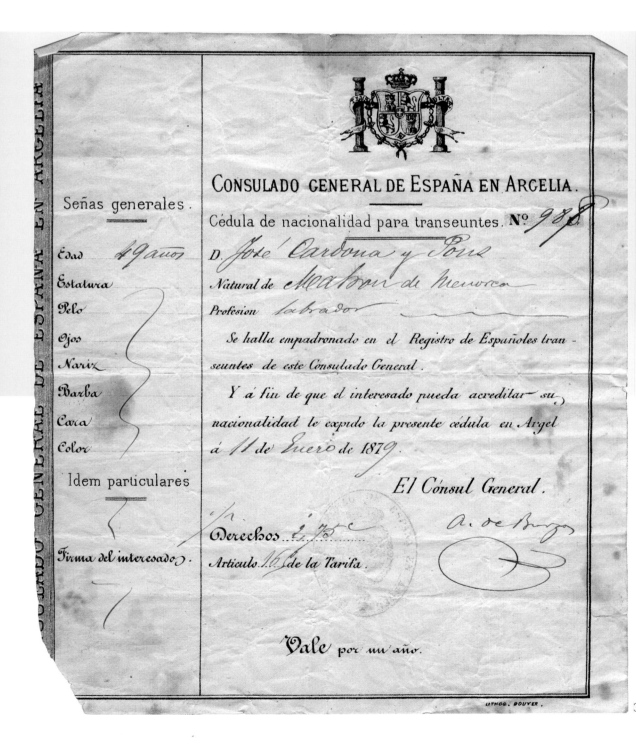

3

4

1- Camus's uncle, Étienne Sintès (right), from whom the boy learned about the hunting, fishing and the sea.
2- Camus (seated, centre), aged 7, in his uncle's cooperage. Étienne is behind him, standing with his arms folded.
3- The Sintès family, originally from the Balearic Islands, had to renew its Algerian residence permit each year.
4- Catherine, née Sintès, Camus's mother.

"Throughout my life I have tirelessly sought to connect with the Spanish in me, which seems to me to be the true me." *Notebooks 1949–1959, OCIV, p. 1241*

"The Spanish in him was his sobriety and sensuality, his energy and sense of nothingness."
The First Man, Appendices, OCIV, p. 925

1- Ibiza in the 1940s.

2, 6- Birth and marriage certificates of Camus's maternal grandmother.

3- Camus's grandmother, Catherine Sintès. She was to bring up her grandchildren alongside her daughter.

4- Around 1930, a hundred years after its coloniz-ation of Algeria, the French government was concerned principally with exploiting the native workforce and with creating and enlarg-ing villages in order to spread the workforce throughout the country.

5- On Camus's mother's side, his family tree could be traced back to Minorca, the second-largest of the Balearic Islands.

The Mediterranean Sea is a pool that links a dozen countries. The men who shout and sing in the cafés of Spain, the folk who wander about the port of Genoa or along the waterfront at Marseille, and the hardy, inquisitive people who live along our coast, all of them belong to the same family. When we travel to Europe, whether we disembark in Italy or in Provence, we heave a sigh of relief on encountering these unkempt people and their tough and colourful life, which we ourselves know so well. I once spent two months in Central Europe, in Austria and Germany, wondering where the peculiar awkwardness that oppressed me, the dull anxiety that possessed me had come from. I have now realized. People in these countries have always lived buttoned up. They have never let themselves go. They have never known what joy is, as opposed to laughter. Yet it is such nuances that define the term 'country'. A country is not an abstraction for which men rush off to die, but a particular taste for life common to a certain group of people that de-termines whether someone feels like a Genoese or a Majorcan or a Norman or an Alsatian. That is what the Mediterranean is: a certain smell, a certain flavour, which it is pointless to attempt to describe; we can feel it through our pores.

The New Mediterranean Culture, II, Observations, OCI, p. 566

"Rigid in her long black prophetess's dress, ignorant and obstinate, she had at least never known resignation. And more than any other person, she had ruled Jacques's childhood."
The First Man, OCIV, p. 790

"Your mother worked as a cleaner. Who looked after you during the day?
- My grandmother. Strictly."
Interview by Carl A. Viggiani, OCIV, p. 638

5

> "To rescue this poor family from the fate of poor people, which is to disappear into history without leaving a mark. The Silent. They were and still are greater than I."
>
> *The First Man*, Appendices, OCIV, p. 930

4

6

1- Lucien Camus, who died at the Front during the Battle of the Marne on 11 October 1914, from shrapnel injuries.

2- Letter from Algiers Town Hall to Mrs Camus informing her of the death of her husband.

3, 4- Soldiers in the trenches during the Battle of the Marne in 1914. More than 80,000 men were to die at the Front.

5- Camus at the local primary school in Rue Aumérat in 1920.

6- Camus's teacher Louis Germain, who was to give up his time to help the boy prepare for the competitive examination for a scholarship to study at a *lycée*. Camus was bright and inquisitive and gained high marks, although the world of education was not to be for him.

7- Correspondence between Camus and Louis Germain following Camus's award of the Nobel Prize in 1957.

8- Good conduct certificate awarded to Lucien Camus of the French Zouaves.

"No, he would never know his father, who would forever rest far away, his face buried in the ashes."
The First Man, OCIV, p. 860

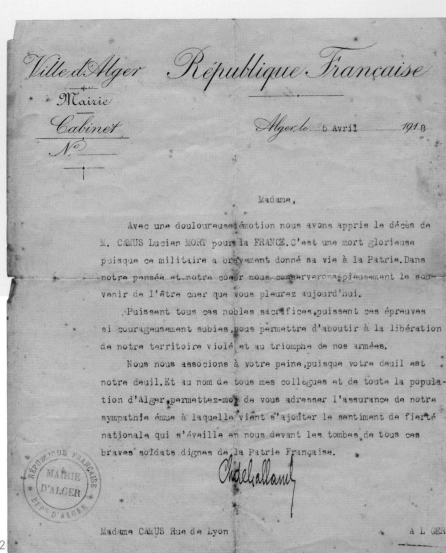

"Mobilization. When my father was called up to serve under the French flag, he had never seen France. He saw it and was killed. (See what a humble family like mine gave to France.)"
The First Man, Appendices, OCIV, p. 922

5

I have let the noise around me in the last few days die down a little before turning to you with an open heart. I have been given far too great an honour, one that I have neither strived nor prayed for. But when I received the news my first thought, after my mother, was of you. Without you, without your loving hand, offered to the poor child I once was, without your teaching and example, none of this would have happened. I dislike the fuss associated with this kind of honour. But at least this is an opportunity to tell you what you were and still are to me, and to assure you that the effort, work and generosity you have shown are still alive in me, your pupil, who in spite of his age, remains your grateful student. I embrace you with all my heart.

Letter by A. Camus to L. Germain, 19th November 1957

I cannot express the joy that both your charming gesture and expression of thanks have given me. If it were possible, I would hug the big boy who you have become very tightly; for me, you will always be "my little Camus".

Letter by L. Germain to A. Camus, 30th April 1959

6 7

"[...] your efforts, your hard work and the generosity with which you undertook them are still fresh in the mind of a little schoolboy who, despite the passing years, has never ceased to be your grateful pupil."

Letter from Albert Camus to Louis Germain, 19 November 1957

"Throughout my career I believe I have respected what is most sacred in children: the right to find their own truth."

Letter from Louis Germain to Albert Camus, 30 April 1959

Cormery went up to the stone and looked at it absent-mindedly. Yes, it was his name all right. He looked up. Small grey and white clouds were passing against the pale sky, which shed an alternately clear and opaque luminosity. All around him, in the vast field of tombstones, there was silence [...]. It was then that he noticed his father's date of birth on the stone and realized that he had never known what it was. Then he read both dates, '1885–1914', and subtracted one from the other mechanically: twenty-nine. Suddenly a thought came to him that sent a shudder through his body. He was forty. The man who was buried beneath this stone, the man who had been his father, was younger than he was.

The First Man, OCIV, p. 754

8

"Along with the other football addicts, he rushed out onto the concrete courtyard, which was surrounded by arcades lined with heavy pillars (behind which the studious and the bookish paraded garrulously) [...] running headlong with the ball at his feet, now avoiding a tree, now dodging an opponent, he thought himself the king of the court and of life."

The First Man, OCIV, p. 877

1- Camus joined the Racing Club of Algiers. Here he is at the front, wearing a cap.

2- In 1953, Camus became a supporter of the Racing Universitaire d'Algérie club, as this membership card shows.

3- Camus in 1941, in the front row, third from the left.

4 to 6- Camus at the Parc des Princes in Paris on 23 October 1957, six days after the announcement of his Nobel Prize.

7- Marcel Cerdan in 1939. Camus often went to boxing matches, which were then popular in Algeria.

8- An article by Camus in the sports weekly *Le RUA* of 15 April 1953.

"On the evening of the fight with Munoz everything followed the usual ritual [...]. He threw himself at Munoz, showering him with a hail of punches [...]. However, [...] when he turned round, his heart was gripped by a dreary sadness at the sight of defeat on the face of the man he had beaten. He understood then that war is bad, because it is just as painful to defeat a man as it is to be defeated."

The First Man, OCIV, pp. 835–836

Carl A. Viggiani: Did you play any stage roles at the *lycée*?

Albert Camus: No, I played football.

Interview by Carl A. Viggiani, OCIV, p. 643

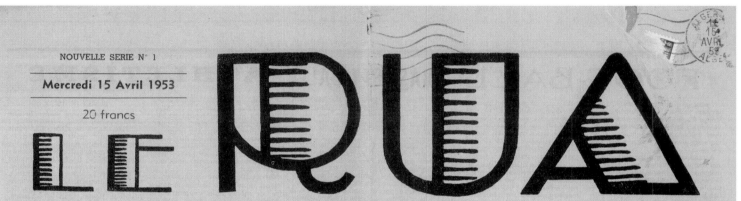

NOUVELLE SERIE N° 1

Mercredi 15 Avril 1953

20 francs

LE RUA

HEBDOMADAIRE SPORTIF UNIVERSITAIRE *publié par* "ALLEZ-RUA"

ORGANE DU RACING UNIVERSITAIRE D'ALGER, SECTION SPORTIVE DE L'A. G. DES ETUDIANTS

REDACTION - ADMINISTRATION : 10, Boulevard Baudin, 10 ALGER

« Le RUA est ma cinquième Faculté ». M. TAILLART, Recteur de l'Université d'Alger

Fondateurs : P. de ROCCA-SERRA, P. PERRIAU — Rédacteur en chef : Ed. BRUA.

Le "R.U.A." ressuscite

PARCE que le journal « LE RUA » ressuscite, il y aura des « falsos » pour dire : « Tiens, parbleu ! Le club traverse une crise grave. Son équipe première est dernière dans le championnat de football, qui gagne le basket, qui pollue les eaux de la natation. C'est pourquoi les dirigeants décrètent le « RUA en danger ! »

Ceci est faux et tout le monde le sait.

Le vrai, c'est qu'il y a une crise grave qui met en danger l'existence du Sport amateur. Une gangrène qui ronge tout le football, qui gagne le basket, qui pollue les eaux de la natation.

Le vrai, c'est que le « RUA » est à peu près le seul club à refuser — héroïquement — de s'embourber dans ces terrains marécageux et de nager dans ces eaux troubles.

Le vrai, c'est que s'il est en queue du championnat départemental, c'est parce que, dans un monde sportif à l'envers, il est à la pointe du bon combat.

Mais une telle lutte, qui semble si naturelle et si facile aux anciens, nourris de pur idéal et de glorieux souvenirs, peut à de certains moments déconcerter et même décourager les jeunes, les nouveaux venus qui cherchent à comprendre leur époque.

Voilà pourquoi le « RUA » ressuscite.

Il s'est donné pour tâche de mieux éclairer la route suivie jusqu'ici par notre grand club universitaire, afin qu'il ne s'y trouve pas de retardataires, afin que jeunes et anciens s'y rapprochent et s'y rassemblent pour marcher d'un même pas, d'un même esprit et d'un même cœur, vers le but commun : la résurrection du Sport pur.

C'est la route droite, la route de l'Honneur sportif. Le « RUA » n'en déviera pas.

« LE RUA ».

L'article du « Toubib »

Depuis 1939, si les Ruaïstes fidèles à leurs traditions, palabraient et chantaient encore, il leur manquait toutefois leur maître moyen d'expression, c'est-à-dire leur journal.

Et, si chez tous, le prurit de la plume ne révélait pas le même caractère d'acuité, chez tous, cependant, s'observaient comme une nostalgie et un amer regret. A tous, les ailes du petit « canard violet » paraissaient définitivement rognées. Plus jamais, semblait-il, il ... avoir conquis, par sa conception du sport, par son respect de la forme, par sa tenue, une juste popularité, essayer de conquérir et persuader plus encore.

Il lui faut, par l'action sur le stade, par la parole et aussi par la plume, sans cesse réaffirmer son désir de totalement ignorer le « sport spectacle » et son corollaire inéluctable : le professionnalisme. S'adressant aussi à ses membres, il doit sans cesse leur redire :

— Rappelez-vous que les victoires ...

La belle époque...

Un article d'Albert CAMUS

Oui, j'ai joué plusieurs années au RUA. Il me semble que c'était hier. Mais lorsqu'en 1940, j'ai remis les crampons, je me suis aperçu que ce n'était pas hier. Avant la finale de la première mi-temps, je tirais aussi fort la langue que les chiens kabyles qu'on rencontre à deux heures de l'après-midi, au mois d'août, à Tizi-Ouzou. C'était donc il y a longtemps. 1928 et la suite, je crois. J'avais débuté à l'Association Sportive Montpensier, Dieu sait pourquoi puisque j'habitais Belcourt et que Belcourt-Mustapha, c'est la Gallia. Mais j'avais un ami, un velu, qui nageait au port avec moi et qui faisait du water-polo à l'ASM. C'est comme ça que se décident les vies. L'ASM jouait le plus souvent au Champ de Manœuvres, sans raison visible la encore. Le terrain avait plus de bosses qu'un tibia d'avant-centre au stade Alenda (Oran). J'appris tout de suite qu'une balle ne vous arrivait jamais du côté où l'on croyait. Ça m'a servi dans l'existence et surtout dans la métropole où l'eau n'est pas franc du collier. Mais au bout d'un an d'ASM et de bosses, on m'a fait honte au lycée. Un « universitaire » devait être au RUA. A cette époque, le velu avait disparu de ma vie. Nous n'étions pas fâchés. Seulement, il allait maintenant nager à Padovani, où l'eau était impure. Pour tout dire, ses raisons n'étaient pas pures, non ? Alors, le velu et moi, on s'était seulement promis de se revoir. Mais les années ont passé. Beaucoup plus tard, j'ai fréquenté le restaurant Padovani (pour des raisons pures) mais le velu s'était marié avec son poids lourd qui devait, selon l'usage, lui interdire de se baigner.

Où en étais-je ? Oui, le RUA. Je voulais bien y entrer, l'essentiel pour moi étant de jouer. Je piétinais d'impatience du dimanche au jeudi, jour d'entraînement, et du jeudi au dimanche, jour de match. Alors va pour les Universitaires. Et me voilà gardien de but de l'équipe junior. Oui, cela paraissait tout simple. Mais je ne savais pas que je venais de contracter une liaison qui allait durer des années, à travers tous les stades du département, et qui n'en finirait plus. Je ne savais pas que vingt ans après, dans les rues de Paris ou même de Buenos-Ayres (oui, ça m'est arrivé) le mot de RUA prononcé par un ami de rencontre me ferait encore battre le cœur, et le plus bêtement du monde. Et puisque j'en suis aux confidences, je puis bien avouer qu'à Paris, par exemle, je vais voir les matches du Racing-Club de Paris, dont j'ai fait mon favori, uniquement parce qu'il porte le même maillot que le RUA, cerclé de bleu et de blanc. Il faut dire d'ailleurs que le Racing a un peu les mêmes manies que le RUA. Il joue « scientifique » comme on dit, et scientifiquement il perd les matches qu'il devrait gagner. Il paraît que ça va changer (d'après Lefebvre), au RUA du moins. Il faut en effet que ça change, mais pas trop. Après tout, c'est pour cela que j'ai tant aimé mon équipe, pour la joie des victoires, si merveilleuse lorsqu'elle s'allie à la fatigue qui suit l'effort, mais aussi pour cette stupide envie de pleurer des soirs de défaite.

J'avais pour arrière le Grand, je veux dire Raymond Couard. Il avait fort à faire, si mes souvenirs sont bons. On jouait dur, avec nous. Des étudiants, fils de leurs pères, ça ne s'épargne pas. Pauvres de nous, à tous les sens, dont une bonne moitié étaient fauchés comme les blés ! Il fallait donc faire face. Et nous devions jouer à la fois « correctement » parce que c'était la règle d'or du RUA et « virilement » parce qu'enfin un homme est un homme. Difficile conciliation ! Ça n'a pas dû changer, j'en suis sûr. Le plus dur, c'était l'Olympique d'Hussein-Dey. Le stade est à côté du cimetière. Le passage était direct, on nous le faisait savoir sans charité. Quant à moi, pauvre gardien, on me travaillait au corps. Sans Roger, j'aurais souffert. Il y avait Boufarik aussi, et cette espèce de gros avant-centre (chez nous on l'appelait Pastèque) qui atterrissait de tout son poids, régulièrement, sur mes reins, sans compter le reste : massage des tibias à coups de crampons, maillot retenu à la main, genou dans les parties nobles, sandwich contre le poteau, etc... Bref, un fléau. Et à chaque fois, Pastèque s'excusait d'un « Pardon, fils » avec un sourire franciscain.

Je m'arrête. J'ai passé déjà les limites fixées par Lefebvre. Et puis je m'attendris. Oui, certes Pastèque avait, du bon. Du reste, soyons francs, nous lui avons rendu son compte. Mais sans tricher, car il est vrai que c'était la règle qu'on nous enseignait. Et je crois bien qu'ici je n'ai plus envie de plaisanter. Car, après beaucoup d'années où le monde m'a offert beaucoup de spectacles, ce que finalement je sais de plus sûr sur la morale et les obligations des hommes, c'est au sport que je le dois, c'est au RUA que je l'ai appris. C'est pourquoi en effet le RUA ne peut pas périr. Gardez-le nous. Gardez-nous cette grande et bonne image de notre adolescence. Elle veillera aussi sur la vôtre.

Albert CAMUS.

Bleu, Blanc et "Lanterne" Rouge !...

Ceci n'est pas une histoire, c'est DE l'Histoire :
Le RUA remportait victoire sur victoire.
(Il était plus finaliste que Leibniz
et faisait de chaque finale un Austerlitz).
Napoléon disait des siennes : « C'est du bronze »
Le Toubib le disait en parlant de son onze.
On était plus ruaiste que le Caïd RUA...

En passant

En prenant aujourd'hui la plume pour aider à la résurrection de la modeste feuille violette à laquelle, il y a quelque vingt ans, certains de ceux que je considérais alors comme des aînés un peu fous s'étaient voués, je pense à mes jeunes camarades Ruaïstes qui, eux aussi, souriront à l'initiative présente des « un peu fous » d' Al-

Economie politique

1) Gide
2) Histoire des doctrines économiques

As far as universities are concerned, I would like them to concentrate on the essentials: teaching intellectual honesty and fostering an appetite for dialogue. If you believe, like Hegel and all subsequent philosophers, that man is subordinate to history and not the other way round, it is impossible to believe in dialogue. You believe in efficiency and the prerogative of power; in other words in silence and lies. You may even believe in murder.

A Way of Life, OC I, p. 673

"In any case, he could not talk to anyone at the *lycée* about his mother and his family, and he could not talk about the *lycée* to anyone at home." *The First Man,* OCIV, p. 893

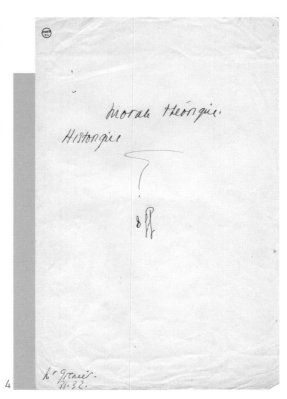

"What drew me to these young people, who had been entrusted to me, was what I could learn from them, rather than what they were supposed to be learning from me."

Memoirs, Jean Grenier

1- The *Lycée Bugeaud* in the centre of Algiers.

2- Camus at 15 (front row, second from left) at the *Lycée Bugeaud.*

3- The front page of the young Camus's political economics notes.

4- The front page of Camus's notes on the theory of morality, which was taught by Jean Grenier.

5- Camus's aunt and uncle, Antoinette and Gustave Acault, outside their butcher's shop in the Rue Michelet in Algiers. A freemason, Gustave Acault let the adolescent Camus explore his collection of books. Camus would say of him: "He was the only man who made me realize what it might be like to have a father."

6- Letter to Mme Camus reporting the good behaviour and work of her son.

5

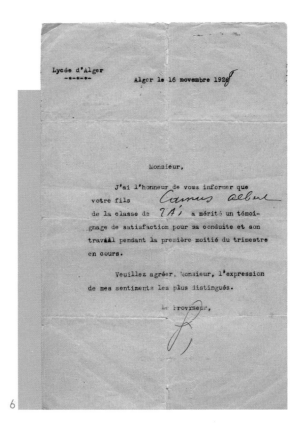

6

"This country does not teach. It neither promises nor suggests. It simply gives, in abundance. It exposes itself shamelessly to our eyes so that we know it intimately as soon as we look at it." *Nuptials, Summer in Algiers*, OCI, p. 117

25. ALGER — Jardins d'essais - Allée des Palmiers

26. ALGER. — *Notre-Dame d'Afrique.* — LL.

Jardin d'essai (jardin d'hiver)

"Walking along the main path, lined with flowerbeds and punctuated by water features, that led down to the sea, they pretended to be casual and civilized under the mistrustful gaze of the guards. But when they reached the first cross-path, they turned towards the eastern part of the gardens, making their way between rows of vast mangroves, planted so close together that hardly any light penetrated them, towards the great rubber trees, whose tumbling branches, growing towards the ground, mingled with their roots, and finally to their real goal, the tall coconut palms at the top of which clustered small, round, orange fruit, which they called *cocosses*."
The First Man, OCIV, p. 768

He was coughing up blood. "My son's lungs have had it," said his mother, without much emotion. It was the age for it. He was seventeen. One of his uncles said he would take care of him, but he was sent to hospital. He spent only one night there, but that one, sleepless, night, spent coughing and spitting and inhaling vile smells, was enough to make him realize just how cut off he was from the real world, where "the others" were happy and healthy. When his mother came to collect him in the morning, more than on any other morning, he was struck by the hopelessness of the world, disguised by the beauty of its surface.

Back and Front, OCI, p. 86

1- The church of Notre-Dame d'Afrique, overlooking Algiers and the Mediterranean: the city's "lighthouse".

2 to 4- The Jardin d'Essai in Algiers.

5- In December 1930, at the age of 17, Camus shows the first signs of tuberculosis. In the spring of 1934, it spreads to his other lung.

"You fell ill in 1930. When exactly?

– In December, I think.

– Did you yourself think or were you told that you might die from your tuberculosis?

– I thought I might. And given the extent of my hemoptysis, I could read the same fear in the doctor's face."

Interview by Carl A. Viggiani, OCIV, p. 643

41 ALGER. — *Vue dans le Jardin d'Essai.* — LL.

4

"Adolescence – vitality and faith in life. But he is coughing up blood. Is that what life is to be? Hospitals, death, isolation? How absurd. This leads to confusion. Yet deep inside him he hears: 'No, no, this is not life'."

The First Man, Notes and Outline, OCIV, p. 942

"The crucial thing as regards what follows is that at that moment on that evening I had accepted the idea, without really thinking about it, that I was going to die and I was thinking like a condemned man rather than like a living being: how long that state of mind lasted is unimportant."

No Tomorrow, 17 March 1938, OCI, p. 1198

5

"The arrival of summer had filled the port with noise and sunlight. It was half past eleven. The day was splitting down the middle, the full weight of its oppressive heat crashing onto the quayside. In front of the warehouses of the Algiers Chamber of Commerce, sacks of corn were being loaded onto freighters with black hulls and red funnels, and fine dust mingled with the choking odour of tar bursting from the ground under the hot sun. Men were drinking at a hut smelling of varnish and pastis while Arabs in red leotards danced on the burning paving stones, their acrobatics mirrored by the twitching of the light on the sea behind them."

A Happy Death, OCI, p. 1108

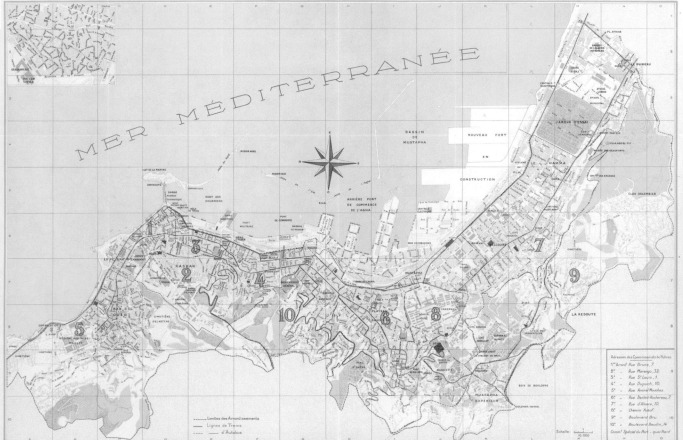

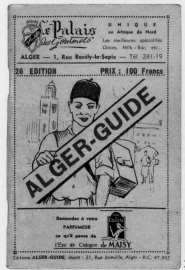

"The office is on the seafront and we spent a few moments watching the freighters in the port, melting in the heat." *The Outsider, OC1, p. 155*

1- Poster commemorating the centenary of colonization. Camus was 17 and studying literature.

2, 3- Map of Algiers and guide to the city. Making his way each day from the poor district of Belcourt to the Lycée Bugeaud, Camus crossed the capital, with its back to the hills and its arms opened to the sea.

4- The Boulevard de la République, which runs along the seafront.

5- Panorama of the port of Algiers, known as "Alger la blanche" (White Algiers).

37 ALGER - Boulevard de la République et Square Bress

LETTER TO JEAN DE MAISONSEUL
8 July 1937

There are so many things I want to say, Jean. I've never cared much about my illness. I used not to understand when you kept telling me that you were sometimes terrified of being run over in the street before you'd had the time to make your mark. Now I understand, because I want to make my mark. I'm working hard. That's what I'm living for, that's the most important thing. Don't you think it's wonderful, Jean, that life is so full of passion and pain?

I'm happy to be seeing you again soon. You'll be able to tell me about everything you've been doing. I remain your faithful friend.

A. CAMUS.
29 Avenue de l'Oriental, Algiers.

"I was living a difficult but at the same time somehow joyous life. I felt as if I could do anything [...]"

Back and Front, Preface, OCI, p. 32

"Did you study the Greek language and literature?
– Not at the *lycée*. I needed it for my teaching diploma so I did a crash course later, at university. Off my own bat I read everything in Greek that I found exciting."
Interview by Carl A. Viggiani, OCIV, p. 640

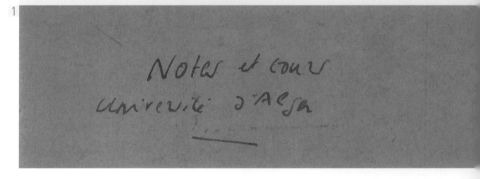

1

2

3

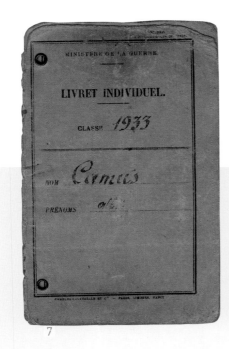

"My illness cut me off [...]"
"I was refused outright a medical certificate to be a teacher."
Albert Camus to Jean Grenier

1-   Jean Grenier in Naples
     in 1926. Through him,
     the young Camus discov-
     ered Marcel Proust and
     André de Richaud. In his
     Reading Notes of April
     1933, Camus also refers
     to Russian literature and
     Spanish writers.

2-   A collection of essays
     by Jean Grenier. In his
     preface to the 1959
     edition, Camus wrote of
     "The shock of reading it
     and the influence it had
     on me [...]"

3, 4- Studio photograph
     of André de Richaud,
     author of *La Douleur
     (Pain)*, published in 1931.

5-   André Gide in around
     1935. Gide remained
     Camus's friend through-
     out his life and Camus
     was to quote him: "I
     wanted to be happy as
     if it was the only thing I
     wanted to be."

I scrutinized my weaknesses but I can honestly say that they did not include the most common fault in men, namely envy, which is a veritable cancer at the heart of every society and every doctrine.

I take no credit for this happy deficiency. I owe it primarily to my illiterate family, who lacked almost everything but envied others almost nothing. It is from its silence, its reserve, its natural and unassuming pride that I learned my greatest and most lasting lessons.

Back and Front, Preface, OCI, p. 32

"I discovered that a poor child could learn to express and free himself through art."

Interview by Carl A. Viggiani, OCIV, p. 643

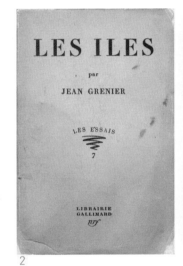

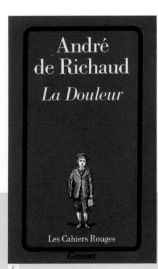

5

"I don't know André de Richaud. But I will never forget his beautiful book, which was the first book that spoke to me about the things I knew: my mother, poverty, beautiful evening skies. It untangled deep inside me a knot of confused threads and removed obstacles whose presence I could feel without being able to name them."

Meetings with André Gide, OCIII, p. 881

"I admire Gide even more after reading his diary. He is so human, isn't he. I still prefer him to all other writers."

Letter from Albert Camus to Jean Grenier, 1932

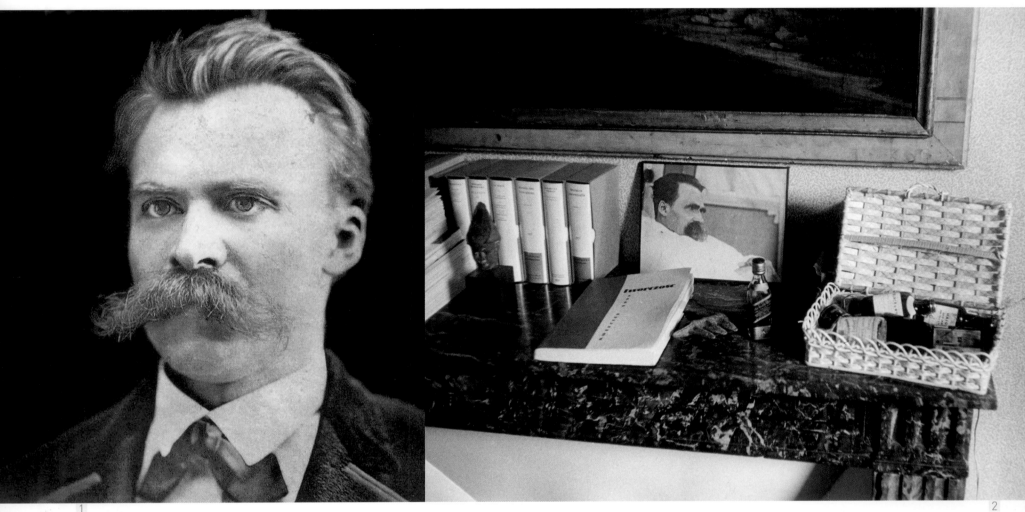

1

2

When I lived in Algiers, I always looked forward to winter because I knew that one night – a single, cold, clear February night – the almond trees in the Vallée des Consuls would burst into white blossom. And I was always amazed to see how these fragile snowflakes withstood the rain and the wind coming in from the sea. Yet every year they did so, which they had to if there were to be any almonds. [...]

This world is poisoned by calamity and seems to delight in it. It abandons itself to this evil, which Nietzsche called oppression. [...]

Where are the triumphant virtues of the human spirit? Nietzsche himself identified them as the mortal enemies of oppression. For him, they were force of character, taste, the "world", traditional happiness, stubborn pride and the cold frugality of wisdom. These virtues are needed now, more than ever, and each of us should choose the one that suits us best. Given the enormity of the stakes, let us not allow ourselves to forget force of character. I am not referring to the force that manifests itself during election campaigns through grimaces and threats, but of the vigour that makes white flowers withstand wind and rain. During this winter into which the world has been plunged, it is that vigour which will bear fruit.

Summer, The Almond Trees, OCIII, p. 587

"Nietzsche could think only in terms of a future apocalypse, not in order to extol it, for he foresaw the sordid, calculating form it would eventually take, but in order to forestall it and to transform it into a new departure."

The Rebel, OCIII, p. 116

"I will return your photograph of Nietzsche. Thank you. It was a great help to me. If you have the chance, perhaps you would take a photograph of it for me, so that I can keep it in the secret archives of my heart."

Letter from René Char to Albert Camus, 13 March 1957

"Here is the Nietzsche photograph! It's an extraordinary document, insignificant yet marvellous, which touches the heart. Keep it in your archives."

Letter from Albert Camus to René Char, 1958

nrf

Copeau, seul maître

Jacques Copeau a beaucoup agacé ses contemporains. Il suffit pour le savoir de lire ce qui s'est écrit à propos de son entreprise. Mais je ne suis pas sûr qu'il n'agacerait pas encore plus aujourd'hui. Il a pris position en effet sur tous les problèmes qui se posent à nous et ses positions ne feraient pas plaisir. Ce qu'il a dit des theatres d'argent est toujours valable, a ceci près que les animateurs de ce theatre sont devenus plus susceptibles à mesure qu'ils devenaient moins compétents et nous assassineraient de communiqués vengeurs si l'on osait reprendre le langage de Copeau. Mais le theatre d'art ne s'en meurt pas pas heureux. Copeau plaçait le texte, le style, la beauté *avant toute chose* et il prétendait en même temps qu'une œuvre dramatique devait réunir, et non diviser, dans une même émotion et un même rire, les spectateurs présents. Loin de pièces sans style, que s'ouvrent de patronage riches de leur seule puissance, que s'entreprise de démolition de la dérision, qui aujourd'hui le transforment impitoyable!

Paris, 17, rue de l'Université — 5, rue Sébastien-Bottin (VIIᵉ)

"I spent a fascinating hour with a frenetic, chaotic person, who twitches constantly but has a dazzling mind."
Albert Camus, A Life by Olivier Todd, Gallimard, 1996

Carl A. Viggiani: "What books on the theatre had you read before founding the Théâtre du Travail?"
Albert Camus: "One by Jacques Copeau, that's all. I still think he is the greatest theatre reformer – and he is my master as far as writing for the stage is concerned."
Miscellaneous Writing, OCIV, p. 644

1, 2- Camus always kept a photograph of Nietzsche with him. The one on the right is on the mantelpiece of his home in Rue Chanaleilles. On the back of it Camus wrote: "Photo of Nietzsche after he went mad [...] I often look at it and I find it curiously encouraging." This is the photograph he slid under the door of his neighbour, René Char, as a token of friendship.

3- Camus's homage to Jacques Copeau.

4- Jacques Copeau, who, with André Gide, helped to launch *la Nouvelle Revue française*. But it was his writing on the theatre which most impressed Camus: "There are two periods in the history of French theatre: before and after Copeau."

5- André Malraux. When he was told that he had won the Nobel Prize, Camus declared: "Malraux should have won it."

"Young love on the beach – and dusk falling over the sea – and stars in the night." *The First Man,* Appendices, OCIV, p. 922

"A stream of fresh water, clear and precious, glinting like a rainbow as it slips by. Plunge your hands into it and you would feel the current clinging to your fingers even as it slid between them. A million instants dying and being reborn, a self-renewing miracle, this stream enchants me. Its voice is the voice of our fairy, who sang without knowing it, with the music of her movements and her gestures."
The Book of Melusine, OCI, p. 989

1- Simone Hié, Camus's first wife. After their separation, Camus remained in contact with her mother, Mme Sogler, and he dedicated two works to Simone: *The Book of Melusine* and *Voices from the Poor District.*

2- Villa belonging to the family of Simone Hié in the Sept Merveilles district of Algiers. The couple lived there during 1934.

3- The ancient site of Tipasa on the Algerian coast.

4- Mireille Bénisti, Simone Hié and Camus among the ruins at Tipasa.

5- Camus and Simone Hié.

3

We had taken only a few steps before the worm-wood grabbed us by the throat. Like grey linen, it covers the ruins as far as the eye can see. Its nectar ferments in the heat, and it is as if the whole world is emitting an intoxicating perfume that rises from the ground towards the sun and befuddles the sky. We walk forward into the arms of love and desire. We are not here to learn or to adopt the acerbic philosophical air expected of us in the face of grandeur. Other than the sun, the wild odours and our own kisses, everything seems futile. I never come here alone. I have often been with people I love and seen on their faces the bright smile that is the expression of love. Here, I leave others to contemplate order and reason. My whole being is overwhelmed by the promiscuousness of nature and the sea.

Nuptials, Nuptials at Tipasa, OCI, p. 106

4

5

1- *Sud*, whose driving force
was Jean Grenier, was a
"monthly review of art and
literature" launched in
1931 by the *lycée* philoso-
phy class, of which Camus
was a member.

2 to 5- Camus's nine exercise
books, collections of
thoughts and ideas, were
published by Gallimard in
three volumes under the
title *Notebooks*. Here are
the cover and a handwrit-
ten page of the first exercise book and two typed
pages from the seventh.

6- Camus acted with the
Radio Alger drama group,
using the stage name
Albert Farnèse. Here
(extreme left) he is playing
the part of Olivier le Daim
in Théodore de Banville's
Gringoire.

7- Camus presented the literary programmes on Radio
Alger. Here he announces
an "interesting and revela-
tory" conference featuring
the writer Claude Aveline.

"I now know that I will be a writer. [...] But
I will write about happiness, even if it is
sometimes harsh. I need to write just as I
need to swim, because my body demands it."

Notebooks 1935–1948, OCII, p. 811

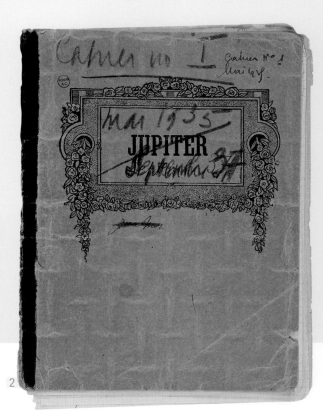

2

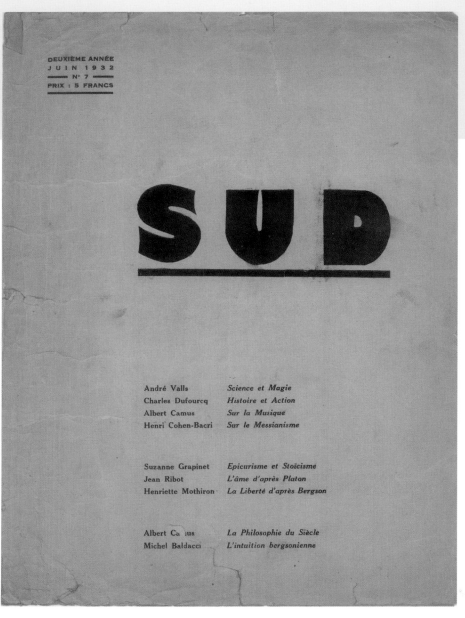

DEUXIÈME ANNÉE
JUIN 1932
N° 7
PRIX : 5 FRANCS

SUD

André Valls	*Science et Magie*
Charles Dufourcq	*Histoire et Action*
Albert Camus	*Sur la Musique*
Henri Cohen-Bacri	*Sur le Messianisme*
Suzanne Grapinet	*Epicurisme et Stoïcisme*
Jean Ribot	*L'âme d'après Platon*
Henriette Mothiron	*La Liberté d'après Bergson*
Albert Camus	*La Philosophie du Siècle*
Michel Baldacci	*L'intuition bergsonienne*

1

3

L'injustice hypocrite amène les guerres. La justice violente
les précipite.

Le marxisme fait à la société jacobine et bourgeoise le
même reproche que faisait le christianisme à l'hellenisme: in-
tellectualisme et formalisme.

Pièce. Il rentre de la guerre. Rien de changé sauf ceci
qu'il ne parle que poétiquement.

Emerson: Tout mur est une porte.

Ne jamais ~~xxxxx~~ attaquer personne surtout dans des écrits.
Le temps des critiques et de la polémique est fini. Création.

Supprimer totalement ~~illxxiiiyxxxi~~ la critique et la polémique
Désormais, la seule et constante affirmation.

Overbeck a eu l'impression que la folie de Nietzsche était
une simulation. Impression que m'a toujours donné n'importe quel
dément. L'amour peut-être est ainsi. Pour moitié, une simulation.

La " limite " doit être la vérité de tous. Elle est la
mienne dans la mesure où je suis à tous, Mais pour moi seul: la
vérité qu'on ne peut pas dire.

Guilloux, de Chamson: " Pour lui, l'autre n'est que l'inter-
rupteur possible "

4

6

Mai - Que la vie est la plus forte - vérité, mais principe de tout
les lâchetés. Il faut penser le contraire ostensiblement.

Et les voilà qui meuglent: je suis ~~immoraliste.~~

Traduction: j'ai besoin de me donner une morale. Avoue-le
donc, imbécile. Moi aussi.

L'autre cloche: il faut être simple, vrai, pas de littéra-
ture - accepter et se donner.

Mais nous ne faisons que ça - Si on est bien
de désespoir, il faut agir comme si on espérait- ou se
tuer.

Intellectuel ? oui. Et ne jamais renier. Intellectuel=
celui qui se dédouble. Ca me plaît. Je suis content d'être les
deux. Question pratique. Il faut s'y mettre.
" Je méprise l'intelligence "
Je préfère tenir les yeux ouverts.

5

Chers auditeurs,

On annonce la venue à Alger de l'écrivain Claude Aveline.
Vous le connaissez tous peu ou prou. Louis Martin-Chauffier nous le
présente comme « Un grand garçon mince, un peu courbé, à l'air doux et
presque timide, parlant sans violence... mais persuasif et charmeur. »
C'est l'influence de Anatole France qui amena Claude Aveline à la littéra-
ture et à l'action. Éditeur, en même temps qu'essayiste, c'est seulement
après avoir connu le vieil écrivain que Claude Aveline publia les
ouvrages qui ont fait sa célébrité. " Le prisonnier ", " Madame
Maillart ", " La fin de Madame Maillart ", etc...
On croit d'ordinaire que ce sont les grands sentiments qui font la vie d'un
homme. Et pourtant c'est aux impondérables du cœur, à ses frémissements
subtils et sans cause que nous devons le meilleur et le plus tragique de
nous-mêmes. Cela Claude Aveline l'a compris. S'il s'attache à un être c'est
la fois pour ce qu'il enferme et pour ce qui le renferme. — au prisonnier
tout autant qu'au conquérant—. Des heures tissées tout le long des
battements d'une montre, les mille détails précis qui frangent tous nos
gestes (tapis usés, rideaux de couleur mal définis)... voilà le champs où
creuse la sensibilité d'Aveline.
Le miracle, c'est qu'une pareille sensibilité, si près de se replier, de
se confondre avec le vieil individualisme des symbolistes. ait pourtant
retrouvé le chemin de la vie. Une fois de plus, c'est l'individu qui fait
route vers les hommes. C'est toujours à la faveur d'un raidissement contre
soi qu'on prend conscience de ses vérités secrètes. En se tournant vers
la misère du monde, Aveline a entrevu la fécondité de son propre drame.
C'est une chose émouvante et singulière que de voir une époque si riche en
individus, oser tant de gestes de fraternité. Aveline est de ceux qui loin
de leurs inquiétudes personnelles, tentent de tracer une route vers
l'esprit et la jeunesse du monde.
Ceci explique son œuvre : son ardeur, son âpreté secrète, son mépris et
dans le même temps ses nuances, sa tendresse, et la délicatesse de son
style. Cet équilibre singulier, c'est à Anatole France qu'il en donne tout
le mérite. Aussi pouvons-nous nous attendre à ce que la conférence
annoncée pour lundi prochain à la salle Pierre Bordes sur Anatole France
précisément, soit particulièrement intéressante et révélatrice.

Radio Alger, Vendredi 19 février 1937

7

ESSAI DE CRÉATION COLLECTIVE

RÉVOLTE
DANS
LES ASTURIES

Pièce en 4 actes

e.c.

A ALGER
POUR LES AMIS
DU THÉÂTRE DU TRAVAIL

2

1, 2- In 1935, the year in which
he began his exercise
books, Camus joined
the militant anti-fascist
movement Amsterdam-
Pleyel, which had been
founded two years ear-
lier by Henri Barbusse
and Romain Rolland and
in which the Commu-
nist Party had a major
influence. Camus invited
Jean Grenier to join, at
the latter's own sug-
gestion (though he did
not remain a member
for long), and strength-
ened his involvement by
founding the Théâtre du
Travail. The group pre-
sented a collective work
called *Revolt in Asturias*,
which dramatized a
recent event in Spanish
history – one that her-
alded the Civil War.

3- Autograph page from
Camus's stage adapta-
tion of *Prometheus in
Chains* by Aeschylus.

4, 5- Costume designs by
Louis Bénisti for *Pro-
metheus in Chains*,
which Camus staged in
1936 with the Théâtre du
Travail.

ÉLECTIONS LÉGISLATIVES

PARTI COMMUNISTE

Le Vendredi 10 Avril à 18 h. 30, au Casino
Bastrana, le Parti Communiste presentera
les Candidats de l'Oranie dans une

GRANDE REUNION

Publique et Contradictoire

sous la présidence du Camarade Caillet
candidat communiste à Mostaganem - Perrégaux

Le camarade ZANNETTACCI

candidat, EXPOSERA LE PROGRAMME DU PARTI COMMUNISTE
assisté des Camarades

BEAUVINEAU, candidat communiste à Bel-Abbès   DESRIAUX délégué à la propagande

Nous invitons MM. GATUING et
LAMBERT à venir apporter la
contradiction.

La Réunion commencera à 18 h. 30 précises.

IMP. DU COMMERCE - ORAN   Vu: Le CANDIDAT

1

An attempt at collective creation, shall we say. That
is true. And it is of value for that very reason. As
well as for the experiment to bring to the theatre a
feature that hardly suits it: action. However, if action leads to death, as it does here, that is enough
to create a certain grandeur peculiar to the human
race: absurdity.

This also explains why, if we had had to choose another title, we would have called the play *The Snow*.
I will explain why. In November, snow covers the
Asturian-Galician Mountains and, two years ago, it
fell on our comrades after they had been shot by
the Spanish Foreign Legion. History has not recorded their names.

Revolt in Asturias, OCI, p. 3

3

"At one time – and you are right to remind me – I refused to accept your point of view. I couldn't understand how you could advise me to become a communist and then yourself take up a position in opposition to communism. I didn't tell you this until later because it was only then that I understood your position. But at the time it hurt me too much for me to see things clearly (now, I'm glad to have had the experience). While we're on the subject, let me tell you why I left the Party."

Letter from Albert Camus to Jean Grenier, 18 September 1951

Prométhée Enchainé – Les Oceanides –

"And it is this admirable desire not to divide or exclude that has always reconciled the human heart and its sufferings with the world and its eternal springs."

Summer, Prometheus in Hell, OCIII, p. 592

"The house overlooking the world is not a place where we have fun but a place where we are happy." *Notebooks 1935–1948, OCII, p. 813*

1- Caricature of Camus by himself, sent to Marguerite Dobrenn.

2- Portrait of Camus by Marie Viton, who made the costumes for the Théâtre du Travail.

3- *The House Overlooking the World*, Louis Bénisti's painting of the house rented by Camus, Marguerite Dobrenn, Jeanne Sicard and Christiane Galindo.

4- Camus, aged 23, in his Rue Michelet apartment in Algiers in late 1936.

5- Camus with his dog Kirk – after Kirkegaard – photographed in front of an original lithograph by Raoul Dufy entitled *Bathing Woken* in the "house overlooking the world".

6- A rare photograph of Camus playing an instrument.

I had friends.
A house overlooking the world.
From expansive dawn to prolonged dusk
The day revolved
Around us in silence. (twice)

Where the world stopped
Our friendship began,
A stubborn desire for clarity,
Which is the definition of freedom.
Thus we advanced from day to day. (twice)

But in that vast blue sky
Is laughter, the indifference of the world.
A few hours' friendship.
Life is a fleeting smile.
The wonder of loving what dies. (twice)

A Happy Death, Appendices, OCI, p. 1197

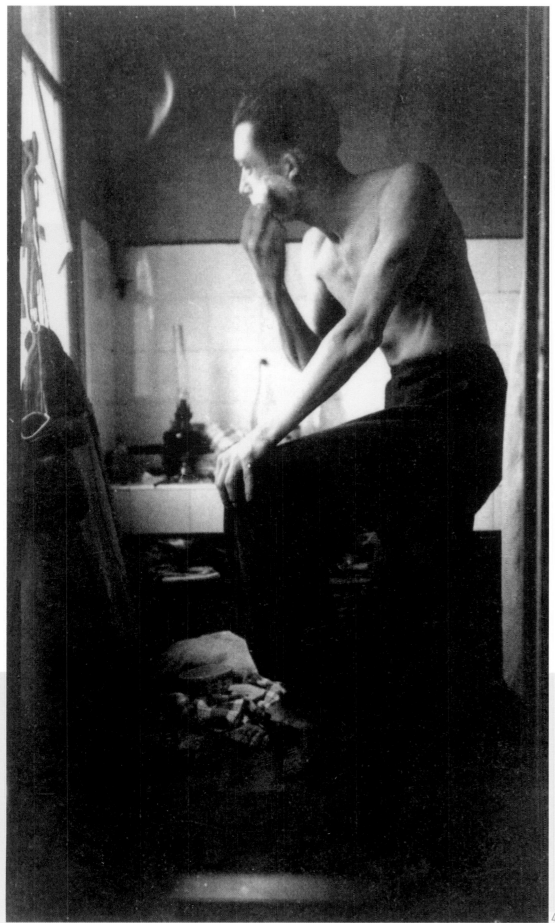

"[...] when the rehearsal was over I saw coming towards us [...] that tall young man, who bowed and held out his hand – a large, open hand, hot and passionate."

Blanche Balain, *The Narrator*, I, autobiographical story covering the years 1937–1939, published by La Tour des vents, 2000, p. 32

1

For the moment, at least, the sound of the incessant breaking of waves on sand came to me through a haze of dancing golden pollen. Sea, countryside, silence, the scent of the earth, all combined in the fragrant vigour that filled me. I bit into the ripe fruit that was the world and was startled by the strong, sweet juice that ran between my lips. No, it was neither me nor the world that was important, but the harmony between us, through which love is silently awakened. And I did not spinelessly claim that love for myself but was eager and proud to share it with my people, a people born of the union of sun and sea, vigorous and sensual, who find grandeur in simplicity and, standing on a beach, meet with a knowing smile the bright laughter of the skies above.

Nuptials, Nuptials at Tipasa, OCI, p. 110

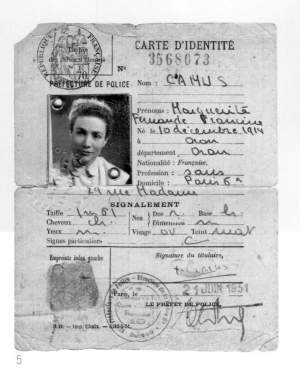

1- After the failure of his first marriage, Camus rediscovered his appetite for life in the company of women.

2- A day at Tipasa in 1935. Camus is with Christiane Galindo (far left) and Madeleine and Robert Jaussaud.

3- In 1937, Camus met Francine Faure, a native of Oran. A pianist and mathematician, she had come to Algiers to study mathematics because women were not admitted to the advanced course in Oran.

4- Marguerite Dobrenn.

5- Francine Faure's identity card. She married Camus in 1940.

"To embrace a woman's body is to embrace the strange joy that radiates from the sky onto the sea." *Nuptials, Nuptials at Tipasa, OCI, p. 108*

"Here I can understand what is meant by 'glory':
the right to love unreservedly." *Nuptials, Nuptials at*
Tipasa, OCI, p. 107

"Go to Tipasa, experience it, and the
work of art will follow. It will free you."
Nuptials, Nuptials at Tipasa, OCI, p. 108

1 to 4-   Camus liked to go with
6 to 9-   friends to Tipasa, 68 km
           west of Algiers, where,
           among the Roman
           ruins that separated
           sky and sea, he could
           breathe freely. These
           visits inspired *Nuptials*
           at Tipasa, *The Wind at*
           Djémila, *Summer in*
           Algiers and *The Desert*.
5-   Camus at Tipasa with
           Christiane Galindo,
           Yvonne Miallon and
           Madeleine Jaussaud.

"In the spring, Tipasa is inhabited by the gods, and the language of the gods is the sun and the scent of wormwood, the sea in its silver armour, the pure blue sky, the ruins covered in flowers and the light gushing from the piles of stones."
Nuptials, Nuptials at Tipasa, OCI, p. 105

"We pause for a moment, mere spectators, before entering the ruined realm."
Nuptials, Nuptials at Tipasa, OCI, p. 106

Sisyphus's silent joy is right here. His destiny belongs to him. His rock is his. The same goes for the absurd man as he confronts his torment and silences every idol he has known. In a universe suddenly restored to silence, Earth's thousand tiny voices can once again be heard, awestruck. Like so many secret and involuntary summons, like guests of every shape and form, they are the obligatory flip side, the reward of victory. No sun without shadow; darkness cannot be denied. The absurd man says yes and never gives up. [...] To him, a godless universe is neither sterile nor futile. To him, every grain of this mountainous rock, every glint from its black surface is a whole world, his own world. The upward struggle is itself enough to fill a man's heart.

The Sisyphus Myth, OCI, p. 303

Awakening and action. 1937–1945

"Faced with the world as it is, I simply do not want to lie or be lied to."

Nuptials, The Wind at Djémila, OCI, p. 115

"[...] a truth is something that grows and strengthens. It is work in progress. And it must be worked at both in writing and in life with determination and a clear head."

No Tomorrows, OCI, p. 1201

1- Camus was responsible
for Éditions Charlot's
Poetry and Drama
series. In it he included
texts from various
cultures and the work of
foreign authors. The col-
lection's visual motif was
created by the famous
architect and draughts-
man Pierre Faucheux, a
friend of Le Corbusier.

2- Edmond Charlot was
only 21 when he discov-
ered Camus, two years
his senior, and decided to
publish *Back and Front*.

3- When Charlot's publishing house ran into dif-
ficulties, Camus teamed
up with his friend Claude
Fréminville to found
Cafre ("Ca" from Camus,
"Fre" from Fréminville).
Together, they were to
publish four works.

4, 5- Charlot's library, called
"True Riches", quickly
became a favourite
meeting place for
Algiers' students.

"Camus set the parameters of what
we should be doing, took on the
collection 'Poetry and Theatre' and
drafted the aims of our 6 principal
collections."

Edmond Charlot in the review *Loess*, nos 18
and 19, January 1985

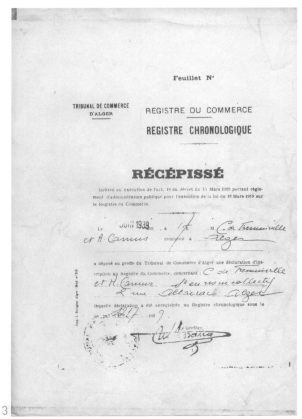

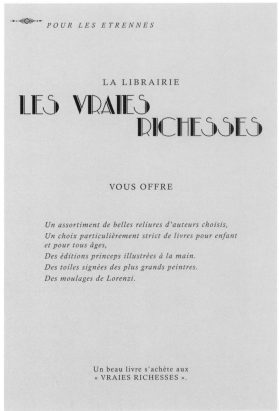

1, 3- In 1937, when Camus was 24, Charlot published *Back and Front*, which was dedicated to Jean Grenier.

2- Autograph title page of *A Happy Death*. In 1938, Camus was working on two novels: *A Happy Death*, which would remain unfinished and be published posthumously in 1971, and *The Outsider*.

4- Chapter title page from *Back and Front*.

5, 6- Autograph pages from *Back and Front*, which Camus reworked several times.

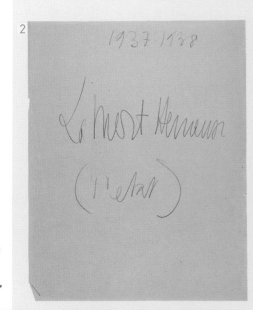

"I find it harder and harder to write. And I find it harder and harder not to write. Nothing is more worthwhile than the effort of writing. [...] I've got lots of ideas and enough work to keep me going for years."
Letter from Albert Camus to Jacques Heurgon, 7 July 1939

"He had sensed the things that tied him to his mother. As if she embodied the vast pity he felt in his heart, which enveloped him and had become real, and, without the slightest pretence, was playing out the role of the poor old woman facing her tragic destiny."
Back and Front, Preface, OCI, p. 51

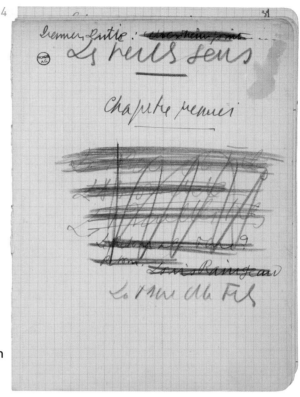

"The essays in this collection were written in 1935 and 1936 (when I was twenty-two) and published a year later, in Algeria. The print run was small. [...] at twenty-two, unless you are a genius, you can hardly write. But [...] there is more genuine passion in these clumsy pages than in all those that followed."

Back and Front, Preface, OCI, pp. 31, 32

Incessantly, it howled through the ruins, swept round a ring of earth and rocks, flooded the piles of pock-marked stones, encircled every column with its hot breath and threw itself wailing into the forum, which was open to the sky. I felt like a mast, slapped by its shrouds. I was bent double, my eyes were burning, my lips were cracking, my skin was so dry it no longer felt part of me. Until then, it had been my interpreter, translating the signs that the world was affectionate or angry, conveying its summer warmth or its winter bite. But now, after being beaten and shaken by the wind for more than an hour, I was numb and weak and was losing consciousness of the messages my body was receiving. Like a pebble washed smooth by the sea, I had been buffed by the wind and was worn to the bone. Increasingly, I had become part of the very force that was buffeting me, until I could no longer distinguish between my own pulse and the violent beating of nature's heart that was everywhere. The wind was shaping me as it had shaped the barren starkness around me. Its invisible grip was fashioning me, like the ancient stones, into a column or an olive trunk standing alone against the summer sky.

Nuptials, The Wind at Djémila, OCI, p. 112

"No, it was neither me nor the world that was important, but the harmony between us, through which love is silently awakened. And I did not spinelessly claim that love for myself but was eager and proud to share it with my people, a people born of the union of sun and sea, vigorous and sensual, who find grandeur in simplicity and, standing on a beach, meet with a knowing smile the bright laughter of the skies above."

Nuptials, Nuptials at Tipasa, OCI, p. 110

1, 2– Autograph pages of *The Wind at Djémila*, part of *Nuptials*.

3– Camus at Bougival in 1945.

4, 5– *Nuptials* was first published in 1939 by Éditions Charlot. Camus was 26. The work is a collection of four lyrical prose poems: *Nuptials at Tipasa*, *The Wind at Djémila*, *Summer in Algiers* and *The Desert*.

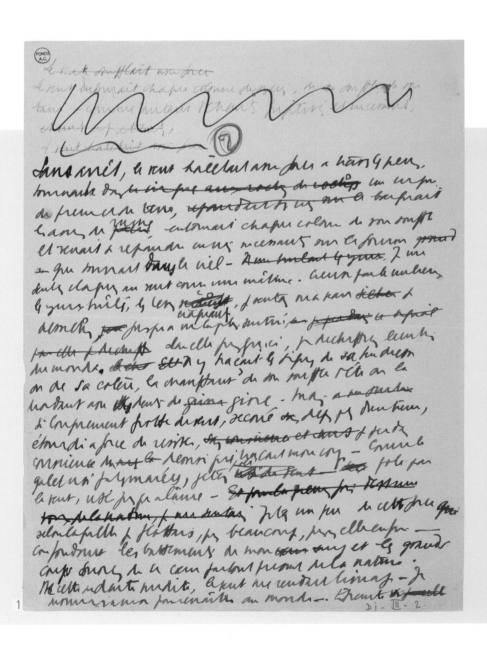

Albert Camus

Noces

essais

ALBERT CAMUS

NOCES

EDMOND CHARLOT
ALGER

The theatre lends itself to dealing with the basic sentiments and emotions that govern human destiny (and only these): love, desire, ambition and faith. But it also satisfies a natural need in the artist, which is for order. It is this tension that makes theatre the ideal medium for both instruction and stimulation. The Théâtre de l'Équipe is founded upon this tension, which means that it will present only works that are honest and simple, in which emotions are violent and the action is cruel. For this reason it will focus on those periods in which love of life was interwoven with hopelessness […].

Manifesto of the Théâtre de l'Équipe, 21 January 1939

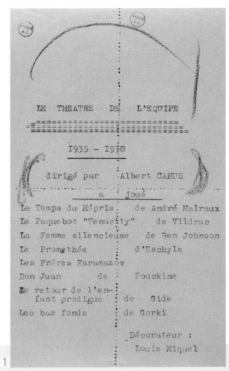

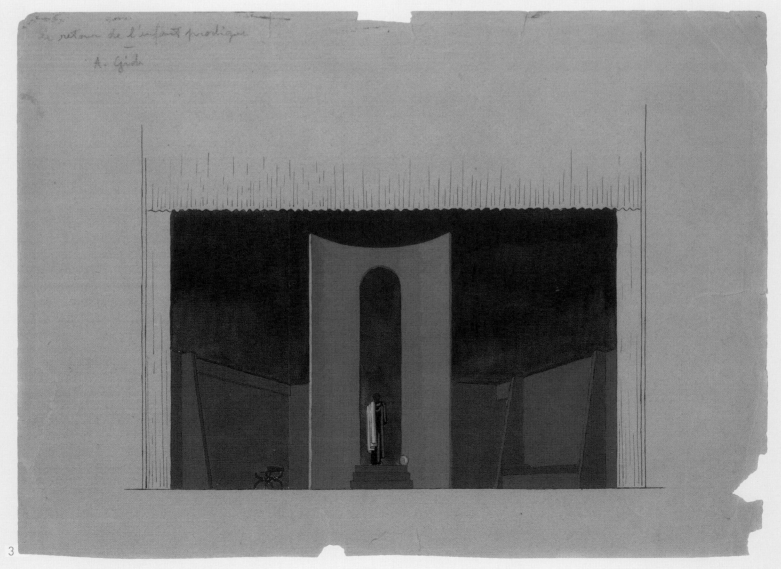

"The Théâtre de l'Équipe has no political or religious axe to grind; it aims to make friends with its audiences." Information on the Théâtre de l'Équipe, OCI, p. 1439

4

5

1, 2, 5– Théâtre de l'Équipe posters and pro-grammes for 1935–1938. Notable is the diversity of playwrights, periods and theatrical styles that the troupe chose to present: Shakespeare's *Hamlet*, Malraux's *Days of Contempt*, Aeschylus's *Prometheus*, Dos-toyevsky's *The Brothers Karamazov*, Rojas's *La Celestina*…

3– Drawing of stage design for Gide's *Return of the Prodigal Son* by Louis Miquel, made after the performances.

4– 1938 performance of Charles Vildrac's *Le Pacquebot Tenacity*, directed by and starring Albert Camus (seated far right).

6, 7– Costume and set designs for Fernando Rojas's *La Celestina* by Louis Bénisti, drawn after the production.

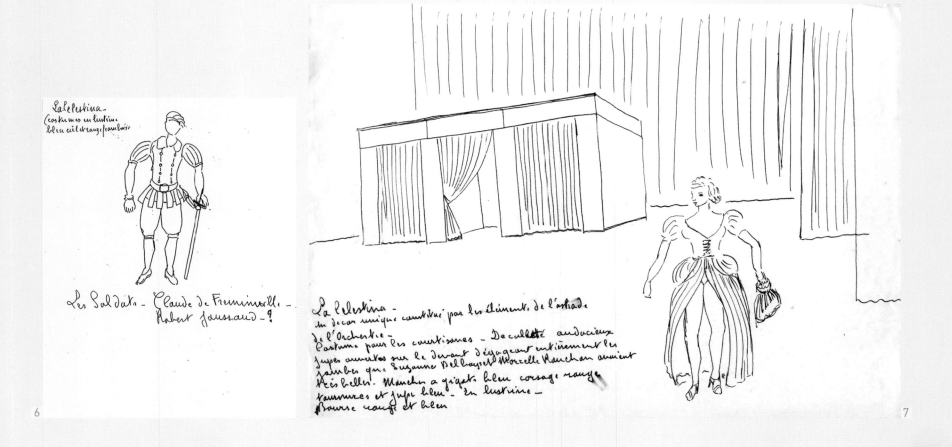

6

7

THE PLIGHT OF THE KABYLES TODAY

I want to talk about poverty. There is no way of avoiding it. It is poverty alone that afflicts the Kabyles today. But this problem gives rise to a multitude of other pressing questions. This is what needs to be understood to put an end to official blathering and reliance on charity.

We have only to look at the facts and figures and to listen to the cries of the Kabyles themselves. We condemn them to their poverty, so we should know what it is like. Overpopulation, pitiful wages, miserable accommodation, lack of water and means of communication, inadequate sanitation and welfare, miserly education; all these factors contribute to the plight of the Kabyle peasants and are the subject of our report.

It is not enough to regard the situation as insoluble. The Kabyles themselves could be excused for thinking so. Some of them expressed this unthinkable wish: "Here's to war, because at least we'd get something to eat." They may think that one absurd situation can cure another, but we know only too well that it is not so and that such wholesale rejection cannot be justified simply in terms of an economic crisis. There are mistakes to be rectified and action to be undertaken.

We shall state our feelings on the matter and we shall do so without restraint. For, as Bernanos said, concealing the truth is not as scandalous as revealing only part of it.

Alger républicain, "The Plight of the Kabyles Today", "Greeks in Rags", 5 June 1939, OCI, p. 655

2

1

"The articles (in *Alger républicain*) cover varied topics, from questions of local democracy to the fight for justice and 'true peace', by way of Algerian political and social emancipation, the plight of the Kabils, the Republican movement in Spain and the ethics of journalism."

André Abbou, *Alger républicain*, OCI, p. 1373

"The Plight of the Kabyles: Among no other people that I know of is the human body subjected to greater humiliation than among the Kabyles [...] the poverty of these people is appalling. [...] If I think of Kabylia, it is not its gorges erupting into flower every spring that come to mind but its procession of blind people and invalids, with hollow cheeks and ragged clothes, which trailed silently behind me all the time I was there."

Alger républicain, "Greeks in Rags", OCI, p. 653

L'AFFAIRE
DES « INCENDIAIRES »
D'AURIBEAU
EN CASSATION

L'histoire d'un crime

ou

Comment on imagine un crime pour les besoins d'une accusation

Voici le texte d'un télégramme qui vient d'être envoyé à MM. le Président de la République, le Président du Conseil, le ministre de l'Intérieur, le ministre de la Justice, le Gouverneur général de l'Algérie et le premier président de la Cour de Cassation, par le Comité de défense des condamnés de Jemmapes-Auribeau :

Organisations soussignées protestent contre verdict rendu par Cour criminelle Philippeville 27 février dernier, à l'encontre ouvriers agricoles Auribeau faussement accusés incendie gourbis inhabités. Stop. Devant absence preuves formelles en raison témoignages douteux et brutalités policières reconnues. Stop. Cour Cassation saisie pourvoi statuera incessamment. Stop. Demandent revision bref délai procès inique.

Union Départementale des Syndicats, Ligue Droits de l'Homme, Parti socialiste, Association Oulamas, Ligue Internationale contre Racisme et Antisémitisme, Fédération nationale Combattants républicains, Bourse Travail Constantine, Parti communiste, Secours populaire, Association républicaine anciens combattants, Comité mondial des Femmes contre la Guerre, Fédération des Elus musulmans, Rassemblement franco-arabe d'Algérie.

Nous donnons aujourd'hui à titre d'information le texte de ce télégramme, non sans l'appuyer de toutes les forces dont nous disposons et de toute notre conviction. Il ne suffit pas cependant de protester. Il faut encore faire protester et éclairer l'opinion publique sur une affaire inadmissible et profondément révoltante.

Dix malheureux ont été condamnés le 28 février 1939 à des peines allant de 6 à 7 ans de travaux forcés. Ils étaient accusés d'avoir incendié des « édifices » lors d'une grève de journaliers agricoles en septembre 1937. Tous sans exception laissent des familles de 5 à 8 enfants dans la misère la plus effroyable.

Et ceci les punis, à la vérité, d'avoir gagné 4 francs par jour pendant des années et d'avoir un jour osé dire que ce salaire ne convenait pas à la dignité d'un homme.

Albert CAMUS.
(Suite de la deuxième page)

P. 2 -- 25-7-39

L'affaire des « incendiaires »
d'Auribeau en cassation

L'HISTOIRE D'UN CRIME

(Suite de la première page)

Mais, pour notre part, nous voulons dire ce que nous savons sur un procès engagé sans aucune preuve que des aveux obtenus, une fois de plus, par des tortures policières et rétractés par la suite. Nous voulons dire ce que nous pensons d'une accusation d'ordre politique, où des innocents sont devenus des incendiaires, où des gourbis de paille ont été transformés en « édifices » et où, par un singulier artifice juridique, un délit justiciable de la prison s'est mué en un crime puni des travaux forcés.

Ce n'est pas la première fois en tout cas qu'une semblable volonté de « frapper fort » se révèle comme le signe le plus certain de l'injustice et du mensonge.

Nous dirons dans de prochains articles l'essentiel de cette affaire en nous bornant à l'exposé des faits et des circonstances. Une fois de plus, nous en ferons juges les hommes de bonne foi de ce pays.

Bien des problèmes de l'heure qu'on nous présente comme essentiels ne valent pas qu'on s'y arrête et ne méritent que le dédain. Mais soixante ans de travaux forcés et la misère de dix familles, cela exige qu'on interroge et qu'on s'interroge.

A l'heure où tant de voix importantes ou supposées telles s'époumonnent pour nous vanter on ne sait quels idéaux de basse qualité, il est plus urgent de mettre tout en œuvre pour freiner l'injustice chaque fois qu'il est possible.

Si la démocratie doit avoir un sens, c'est ici qu'elle le prendra et non dans les discours officiels du dimanche. Et il est permis de supposer que l'innocence reconnue des condamnés d'Auribeau lui fera rattraper le temps et le prestige que la mobilisation morale à sens unique lui a déjà fait perdre en ce pays.

(A suivre.)

A. C.

3

1- The first issue of *Alger républicain*, a liberal daily edited by Pascal Pia, appeared in 1936, just after the formation of the Popular Front party. Camus was 26 when, to supplement his meagre earnings from creative writing and publishing, he started writing for the paper. His articles appeared under the banner "The Reading Room" as well as in the legal section, where he called for equal rights for Muslims, especially the right to social welfare. In a series of articles that ran from 6 to 15 June 1939, Camus denounced the treatment of the Kabyles, whose plight he had witnessed.

2- Camus with the staff of *Alger républicain* in 1938 or 1939.

3- The Auribeau case, in which ten agricultural workers were convicted of arson despite a lack of evidence, outraged Camus, who condemned the decision in the 25 July 1939 issue of *Alger républicain*.

1

3

SILENCE

L'ENNEMI GUETTE VOS CONFIDENCES

PAUL COLIN

2

Je,soussigné,Docteur A Lévi Valensi,médecin des hôpitaux,
certifie donner mes soins à Monsieur Albert Camus depuis
août 1931.
Monsieur Camus était porteur à cette époque d'un pneumothorax thérapeutique gauche qui avait été créé en février
1931 par monsieur le docteur Loubeyre pour une tuberculose
pulmonaire(infiltration de la presque totalité du poumon ga
gauche)d'évolution aigue avec atteinte débutante du sommet
droit.Ce pneumothorax avait donné d'emblée les mailleurs
résultats:chute de la température,négativation de la bacil-
loscopir et reprise importante du poids.
J'ai continué dès lors les insufflations jusqu'en Mai 1938;
pendant tout ce temps,Monsieur Camus n'a présenté aucun in-
cident particulier;il s'est normalement développé et a pu
poursuivre des études secondaires puis supérieures sans
jamais avoir à les interrompre,et en travaillant même en
dehors de ses heures d'études pour subvenir à ses besoins.
            A l'heure actuelle,monsieur Camus ne
présente plus depuis longtemps de signes fonctionnels de
tuberculose;sa températurex est normale,sa bacilloscopie né-
gative(examen du 30 août 1938 pratiqué par Mr le dr Thiode}
;l'auscultation et la radiographie ne montrent que les
séquelles de l'affection dont il a été atteint il yna 7 ans
            Je considère qu'a l'heure actuelle,mon
sieur Camus peut,sans danger pour lui ni pour son entourage
remplir les fonctions d'enseignement auxquelles il désire a
accéder.En foi de quoi,je lui délivre le présent certificat
conforme a la vérité pour valoir ce que de droit.

GOUVERNEMENT GÉNÉRAL   D. 42.849   M/L.   RÉPUBLIQUE FRANÇAISE
DE L'ALGÉRIE

CONTROLE MÉDICAL   Alger, le .10 OCT. 1938   193
DE L'ALGÉRIE
Direction et Contrôle
des Services Médicaux,
                                Le Médecin Contrôleur Général de l'Algérie
Nº 1365   à Monsieur Albert CAMUS

NOTA.— Prière de rappeler, dans la   29 Avenue de l'Oriental   ALGER
réponse, la date et le numéro de la pré-
sente.

            J'ai l'honneur, comme suite à votre lettre du 17 sep-

        tembre dernier, de vous retourner les certificats communiqués.

            J'ai le regret de vous confirmer la communication qui

        vous a été faite en ce qui concerne l'impossibilité de vous

        déclarer indemne de tuberculose, dans le cadre de la règlemen-

        tation en vigueur.

                                        Le Médecin Contrôleur Général de l'Algérie,

Imprimerie Algérienne. — C.M. - Série 300 - Nº 312 - 1938.

pièces jointes

5

"[...] we protested vehemently when the censor proposed to hack bits out of the news pages [...] Of course, censorship is often mindless and almost always mindlessly applied, but believe me, the mindlessness of the censorship system in Algeria was in a class of its own."

Letter from Pascal Pia to André Abbou, December 1970, OCI, p. 866

1- The Wehrmacht marching into Paris on 14 June 1940, the start of the German occupation. General Kurt von Briesen (mounted) is saluting the 30th Infantry Division as it advances down Avenue Foch.

2- Poster designed by Paul Colin as part of the wartime campaign to warn people against discussing confidential information.

3- Petrol coupons. Rationing was introduced in the occupied zone.

4, 5- Despite repeated requests, Camus was denied permission by the government to teach or join the army on account of his tuberculosis.

6, 7- *Alger républicain* followed the German army's conquest of Eastern Europe. On 30 August 1939, a front page article was deleted by the censor: the "Fifth Letter by Vincent Capable, Fruiterer, on the Fate of Simple Men". Vincent Capable was a pseudonym used by Camus. The outspoken reporting of Camus and Pascal Pia offended the powers-that-be and the paper was first censored, then, in September 1939, banned. It became *Le Soir républicain*, with Camus as its editor.

"*Alger républicain* became an evening paper called *Le Soir républicain* and, as luck would have it, I was one of the few writers not called up. [...] I therefore tried to create a newspaper that reflected my idea of the truth. In other words, I upheld the freedom of speech against censorship and war without vitriol (for example, on the subject of negotiating peace) and without propaganda. I must have at least partially succeeded because the paper was banned in January after a long battle."

Letter from Albert Camus to Jean Grenier, June 1940

"On two occasions, following complaints from the military authorities, the paper was ordered to blank out an article and withdraw the issue from circulation, edicts to which Mr Camus and Mr Pia responded in letters declaring that they would no longer accede to the demands of the censor [...]"

Anonymous testimony recorded by Albert Camus

Lyon, le 3 Décembre 40

Vous êtes tous deux si sympathiques
Que nous souhaitons vous voir heureux.
Acceptez donc les meilleurs vœux
D'un "cadratin" typographique.......

    Cornier
    Guénette
    Lemoine
    Lemaître

Lyon

"We liked him even more when we were invited to his wedding. I was touched by the simplicity of the ceremony, with just three or four typesetters in attendance. How about that for a sign of affection! His wife, too, was so simple and kind [...] When we came out of the town hall we went to a café, as if we were just friends meeting for a drink."

Lemaître, *To Albert Camus from his Friends at the Press*, Gallimard, 1962, p. 24

"Touched, he held her close and kissed her as tenderly as he had ever kissed her. She did not resist and for a moment they were as happy as they had been at the start of their marriage."

Exile and the Kingdom, Jonas or the Artist at Work, OCIV, p. 70

1, 2- Francine joined Camus in France and they married on 3 December 1940. Pascal Pia was with them.

3- The typesetters at *Paris-soir* sent their best wishes to the young couple and gave Francine a bouquet of violets. They were to say, in memory of Camus: "He was a real man of the press. We thought of him as a book worker. [...] He worked as if he were at home. He was lively and fun, always joking and always with it, in other words a real old-fashioned editor."

4, 5- Camus and Pascal Pia in Lyon in December 1940. Unable to find work, Camus left Algeria to rejoin Pia, who was working for *Paris-soir*. The paper had quit the capital and set up first in Clermont-Ferrand, then in Lyon.

"I've made up my mind to leave Algiers and go to Paris. I can't find work here."

Letter from Camus to Pascal Pia, 16 February 1940

The typesetter Lemaître recalls:

"My own memory of Camus was of the perfect friend. And he became my friend as soon as we met, which is quite rare."

To Albert Camus from his friends at the Press, Gallimard, 1962

1, 2, 4- In 1941, Albert and Francine Camus returned to Algeria and settled in Oran. They had no regular income. Francine worked as a supply teacher and Camus gave a few lessons in private establishments. Despite their financial difficulties, the couple were happy.

3, 6, 7- Albert and Francine Camus in 1942, at Canastel, near Oran.

5- The Rue d'Arzew in Oran, where the couple had their apartment.

"The most generous legacy is to give everything to the here and now." *The Rebel, OCIII, p. 322*

ORAN. — Rue d'Arzew. Les Arcades.

ND. Phot.

5

6

7

"Within a few seconds they were naked, a moment later plunging into the water, swimming energetically and clumsily, shouting, dribbling and spitting, and seeing who could dive deeper or stay under longer. The water was soft and warm, the sun now easier on their wet heads, and their young bodies were so full of light and radiance that they could not stop screaming with joy. They were the sovereigns of the sea, of life itself. There was no greater treasure the world could offer and they took it and spent it recklessly, like monarchs with absolute rights and limitless wealth."

The First Man, OCIV, p. 770

"The times that are upon us have managed to destroy everything in me except this chaotic appetite for life itself. It is both a productive and a destructive passion. It afflicts me constantly and erupts even in the darkest pages of *Back and Front*." *Back and Front, Preface,* OCI, p. 36

"We were foolish, I suppose. We wanted to act as if the war didn't exist. But it was the war that came between us."
Letter from Francine Camus to Nicolas Chiaromonte, Oran, 31 December 1942

"Like rats!"
Notebooks 1935–1948, OCII, p. 966

1

3

"Yes, what I love about Algerian cities is inextricably linked with the people who live in them. [...]

No, don't go there if you are faint-hearted or soulless. Definitely not! But if you understand the suffering that lies between yes and no, between midday and midnight, the pain of love and rejection, if you simply want to light fires by the sea, there you will find the flame you need."

Summer, Little Guide to Cities without a Past, OCIII, p. 596

4

5

6

"Above Oran is the Santa-Cruz mountain, from which a thousand ravines descend to the plateau. Once passable roads cling to the slopes overlooking the sea."

Summer, The Minotaur or an Hour in Oran, OCIII, p. 582

7

1, 5- Francine and Albert supported and stood by each other throughout their lives.

2- Camus with his friend André Bénichou.

3- Albert and Francine having lunch with their close friends Robert Jaussaud and Manette Martin (Francine's cousin).

4- Camus in Oran in 1941.

6- The Bay of Oran in the 1940s. The country was in the grip of a typhus epidemic, which partly inspired *The Plague,* and life was difficult. Camus decided to go back to France alone.

7- Algerian lottery ticket bought by Albert and Francine.

Then, for some reason, something exploded inside me. I started shouting at the top of my voice and I insulted him and told him not to pray for me. I had grabbed him by the collar of his cassock. I was pouring everything out at him from the bottom of my heart in a paroxysm of joy and anger. He seemed so certain of everything, didn't he? And yet none of his certainties was worth one hair of a woman's head. He couldn't even be sure he was alive because he was living like a dead man. I might seem to be empty-handed. But I was sure of myself, sure of everything, surer than he was, sure of my life and sure of the death that was coming to me. Yes, that was all I had. But at least it was a truth I could hold on to just as it had hold of me. [...] From the depths of my future, throughout the whole of this absurd life I had been leading, I had felt a vague breath drifting towards me across all the years that were still to come, and on its way this breath had evened out everything that was then being proposed to me in the equally unreal years I was living through. [...] As if this great outburst of anger had purged all my ills, killed all my hopes, I looked up at the mass of signs and starts in the night sky and laid myself open for the first time to the benign indifference of the world. And finding it so much like myself, in fact so fraternal, I realized that I had been happy, and that I was still happy. For the final consummation and for me to feel less lonely, my last wish was that there should be a crowd of spectators at my execution and that they should greet me with cries of hatred."

The Outsider, OCI, pp. 211–213

1- *The Outsider* was published by Gallimard in May 1942 and *The Sisyphus Myth* in October of the same year. Camus was 29.

2 to 4- Autograph pages of *The Outsider.*

5- Typescript of the novel with corrections by Camus.

6- André Malraux and Pascal Pia. It was thanks to their efforts that *The Outsider* and *The Sisyphus Myth* – two of the "Absurdities" Camus was working on at the time, along with the plays *Caligula* and *The Misunderstanding* – found their way onto the desk of Jean Paulhan, editor of the *Nouvelle Revue française* at Gallimard.

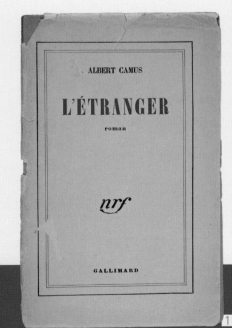

"Finished *Sisyphus.* The Absurdities are finished. The foundations of freedom."
Notebooks 1935–1948, OCII, p. 920

> "So one would not be far wrong in seeing *The Outsider* as the story of a man who, without any heroic pretensions, agrees to die for the truth."
>
> *The Outsider,* Preface to an American edition, OCI, p. 216

"Roland Malraux, André's brother, was in Lyon the other day and I gave him your manuscripts to show to his brother. [...] Naturally, I had already mentioned *The Outsider* and *Caligula* in my letters to Paulhan."

Letter from Pascal Pia to Albert Camus, May 1941

1- In 1967, Luchino Visconti adapted *The Outsider* for the screen. The character of Meursault was played by Marcello Mastroianni.

2- In the film, Anna Karina played Meursault's girl-friend, Marie Cardona.

3- *The Outsider* has been published on every continent and translated into over 60 languages.

4- The artist Mayo, who was part of the Gallimard circle, was asked by Camus to illustrate the second edition of *The Outsider*, which appeared in 1946. From 1942 until 1953, Mayo also designed the sets for the Théâtre des Mathurins, where Camus and he were to cross paths again.

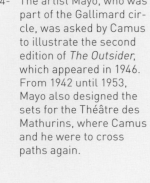

"*The Outsider* is neither realism nor fantasy. I see it rather as a myth in the form of a person, but deeply rooted in the physicality and intensity of everyday life. People have tried to see in it a new kind of anti-morality, which is utterly wrong."

Letter from Albert Camus to Rolf Hädrich, 8 September 1954

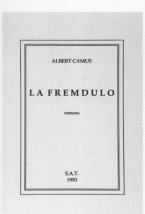

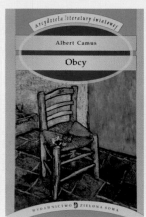

3

4

"What I am attacking here is not morality but the judicial system, whether it is Nazi or communist or simply middle-class, which is nothing less than a social cancer. [...] Meursault is opposed to the judges, the laws of society, conventional sentiments. He simply exists, like the wind or a stone in the sun, and they never lie. If you interpret the book in this light, you will find in it a paean to sincerity and an at once ironic and tragic eulogy to worldly pleasure – and no darkness, no expressionist posturing, no depiction of despair."

Letter from Albert Camus to Rolf Hädrich on the latter's adaptation of *The Outsider* for radio, 8 September 1954

"After trying to get into Spain and giving up because I would have had to spend several months in a camp or a prison, which I couldn't do in my condition, I joined the resistance. I gave it a lot of thought and went into it with my eyes wide open; it was my duty. I operated first in Haute-Loire and then in Paris, where I joined Combat with Pia."

Camus at Combat, edited by J. Lévi-Valensi, Gallimard, 2002, p. 18

3   4

"In fact, the situation affects you; it affects all of us, because the
enemy has now created such a web of links among the French people
that one person's actions have a knock-on effect on everyone else's,
and one person's inattention or carelessness can mean the deaths of
ten others." Underground issue of *Combat*, no. 55, March 1944, OCI, p. 912

1- As a member of Combat,
Camus used a forged
identity card in the name
of Albert Mathé.

2, 5- In 1943, Camus became a
reader for Gallimard and
came into contact with the
underground movement
Combat, for whose news-
letter he wrote several
articles. He wanted to
join the resistance but
his health prevented him
from fighting. His pen was
his weapon and he fought
in the pages of *Combat*,
which was initially an
underground publication
but later circulated freely.
The first article identified
as being by Camus, enti-
tled *Total War Means Total
Resistance*, dates from
March 1944.

3- Camus with the staff
of *Combat*. From left
to right, those present
include: Petit Breton (in
uniform), Victor Peroni,
Albert Camus, Albert
Ollivier (smoking), Jean
Bloch-Michel (in profile),
Jean Chauveau (drinking)
and Roger Grenier (with
glasses, facing the cam-
era).

4- The North African foot-
ball team, entertained by
Camus in the offices of
Combat.

A GUERRE TOTALE
RÉSISTANCE TOTALE

On ne ment jamais inutilement. Le mensonge le plus impudent, pourvu qu'il
soit répété assez souvent et assez longtemps, laisse toujours sa trace. C'est un principe que la propagande allemande a pris à son compte et, nous avons aujour-
d'hui encore un exemple de la façon dont elle l'applique. Inspirée par les services
de Goebbels, aboyée par la presse des domestiques, mise en scène par la milice, une
formidable campagne vient de s'ouvrir qui, sous le couvert d'une lutte contre les
patriotes des maquis et de la Résistance, vise à diviser une fois de plus les Français.
On dit aux Français : « Nous tuons et nous détruisons des bandits qui vous tue-
raient si nous n'étions pas là. Vous n'avez rien de commun avec eux. »

Mais si le mensonge, tiré à des millions d'exemplaires, garde un certain pouvoir,
il suffit du moins que la vérité soit dite pour que le mensonge recule. Et la vérité
la voici : C'est que les Français ont tout en commun avec ceux qu'on veut aujour-
d'hui leur apprendre à craindre et à mépriser. Il n'y a pas deux France, l'une qui
combat et l'autre qui juge le combat. Car quand bien même certains voudraient
rester dans la position confortable du juge, cela n'est pas possible. Vous ne pouvez
pas dire « Cela ne me concerne pas ». Car cela vous concerne. La vérité est qu'aujourd'hui l'Allemagne n'a pas seulement déclenché une offensive contre les meilleurs
et les plus fiers de nos compatriotes, elle continue aussi la guerre totale contre la
totalité de la France, totalement offerte à ses coups.

Ne dites pas « Cela ne me concerne pas. Je vis à la campagne et la fin de la guerre me trouvera dans la paix où j'étais déjà au début de la tragédie. » Car cela vous
concerne. Ecoutez plutôt. Le 29 Janvier, à Malleval, dans l'Isère, tout un village,
sur le seul soupçon que des réfractaires avaient pu s'y réfugier, a été incendié par
les Allemands. 12 maisons ont été complètement détruites, 11 cadavres découverts,
une quinzaine d'hommes arrêtés. Le 18 Décembre en Corrèze, à Chaveroche, à 5 k.
d'Ussel un officier allemand ayant été blessé dans des conditions obscures, 5 otages
ont été fusillés sur place et deux fermes incendiées. Le 4 Février à Grole, dans
l'Ain, les Allemands n'ayant pas trouvé les réfractaires qu'ils recherchaient, ont fu-
sillé le maire et deux notables.

Lire la suite au verso

5

Have you ever seen a man executed by firing squad? Of course not. Such occasions are generally by invitation only and the audience is carefully selected. So all you have to go on are pictures in books: a blindfold, a post and a group of soldiers several yards away. Well, think again! In fact, the squad of riflemen is only five feet from the victim. If he took two steps forward, his chest would be up against the rifle barrels. What is more, the riflemen aim at his heart and, given the number of large-calibre bullets and the distance they have to travel, they make a hole big enough to put your fist through. You did not know any of this because such details are never mentioned. For plague-victims, life is less important than other people's sleep. Good citizens must not be kept awake. That would be in bad taste; good taste is not to force it down people's throats, because everyone already knows. But I have not slept well since that experience. I still have the bad taste in my mouth and I have not stopped forcing it down my throat; I cannot stop thinking about it.

The Plague, OCII, p. 208

"I do not know whether you can adequately visualize the reality behind this stark report. But is it possible not to be outraged and disgusted on reading these bland figures: 86 men; 3 hours?"

Underground issue of *Combat*, "They spent three hours shooting Frenchmen", no. 57, May 1944, OCI, p. 915

"This scene is one that should be kept in front of people so that they never forget, in front of all those French people who are still standing on the sidelines. For among these 86 innocent people were many who thought that because they had done nothing to resist the German forces, nothing would be done to them. But France is a unit: our anger is communal and we are all martyrs."

"They spent three hours shooting Frenchmen", OCI, p. 916

1, 3, 4- Camus in the offices of
          Combat.
2-   The front page of the 57th
          underground issue of
          Combat, dated May 1944.
          Camus was referring to
          the Ascq massacre on
          1 April 1944, when 86
          people were executed.

Time will prove that the men of France did not want to kill and that their hands were unsullied at the start of a war that was not of their choosing. All the more prodigious, then, was their sudden resolution to use those hands to fight, to take up arms and to fire into the dark, night after night, against soldiers who for two years thought war was easy. [...]

It is hardly to be expected that men who have spent four years silently fighting, whole days in the sun amid the fracas of guns, should accept the reestablishment of a regime based on resignation and injustice, in whatever form. We cannot expect our heroes to tolerate today what the great and the good of the last generation contented themselves with for twenty-five years: mute patriotism and tacit disdain for their leaders. The people of Paris who took to the streets this evening are those who would rule it tomorrow. Not to have power, but to institute justice; not for political advantage, but for moral advancement; not to control their country, but to extol it.

We do not believe that this will happen; we believe that it is happening today, through suffering, persistence and struggle. And that is why, despite the pain, the blood and the anger, the random bullets, the arbitrary injuries and the lives lost for ever, it is not regret that we must give voice to, but hope – the daunting hope of men facing their destiny alone.

Camus at Combat, *Bloody Freedom,* 24 August 1944, p. 149
Reprinted in *Our Times I – Chronicles 1944–1948,* OCII, p. 379

1- *Combat* is circulated freely from 21 August 1944 after four years of clandestine publication. Camus is its Editor and Pascal Pia its Publisher. The Pia–Camus team was to give up the reins on 3 June 1947 after running into insurmountable financial difficulties.

2- Autograph title page of *The Minotaur or an Hour in Oran* on *Combat* letterhead. *The Minotaur* would appear first in the review *Arche,* no. 16 of 1946, and then as part of the collection *Summer,* published by Gallimard in 1954.

3- Press card.

4- Camus speaking at a meeting of the National Liberation Movement in 1944. Beside him is Henri Frenay, resistance fighter and one of the founders of *Combat* in 1940.

5- André Malraux, alias Colonel Berger, in the offices of *Combat* on 22 September 1944. On the left are Camus and Jacques Baumel.

6- Celebration of the liberation of Paris in the Place du Châtelet on 26 August 1944.

7- Tax Office card confirming Camus's exemption from entertainment tax.

"It has taken five years of silent and persistent struggle for our newspaper, which was born of the spirit of resistance and was published without interruption despite the perils of maintaining secrecy, finally to emerge into the daylight now that Paris has been freed from its humiliation. It is impossible to write these words without emotion." "From resistance to revolution", *Combat,* 21 August 1944, OCII, p. 516

"Paris is burning its bullets and the flames are illuminating the night sky. Against a vast backdrop of stone and water, on either side of a river heavy with history, the barricades of freedom are once again being erected. Yet again, justice has been paid for with human blood."

Camus at *Combat, Bloody Freedom,* 24 August 1944

Reprinted in *Our Times I – Chronicles 1944–1948,* OCII, p. 379

"It is France's workers and teachers who will define her future. If they go hungry, we will have reason to be ashamed. But if their demands for food and justice are met, our conscience will be clear."

Combat, 5 April 1945, OCII, p. 610

"It is justice that will rescue Algeria from hatred." *Combat*, 23 March 1945, OCII, p. 617

1

"Talking of politics, I would like to reiterate that Arabs are people. By that I mean they are not merely an anonymous mass of peasants with nothing worth fighting for, as the Western world sees them. On the contrary, they are people with great traditions and the highest values, for all our reluctance to assess them impartially."
Camus at Combat, 14 May 1945, p. 499
Reprinted in Our Times III – Algerian Chronicles 1939–1958, OCIV, p. 338

2

"When millions of people are starving, everyone is implicated."

Camus at Combat, 16 May 1945
Reprinted in *Our Times III – Algerian Chronicles 1939–1958*, OCIV, p. 343

"What must be shouted from the rooftops is that most of the population of Algeria is starving."

Camus at Combat, 15 May 1945
Reprinted in *Our Times III – Algerian Chronicles 1939–1958*, OCIV, p. 340

> "Such shameful acts must cease. These
> few have kept honour alive. They alone are
> testaments to courage."
>
> *Combat*, 17 May 1957, OCII, p. 417

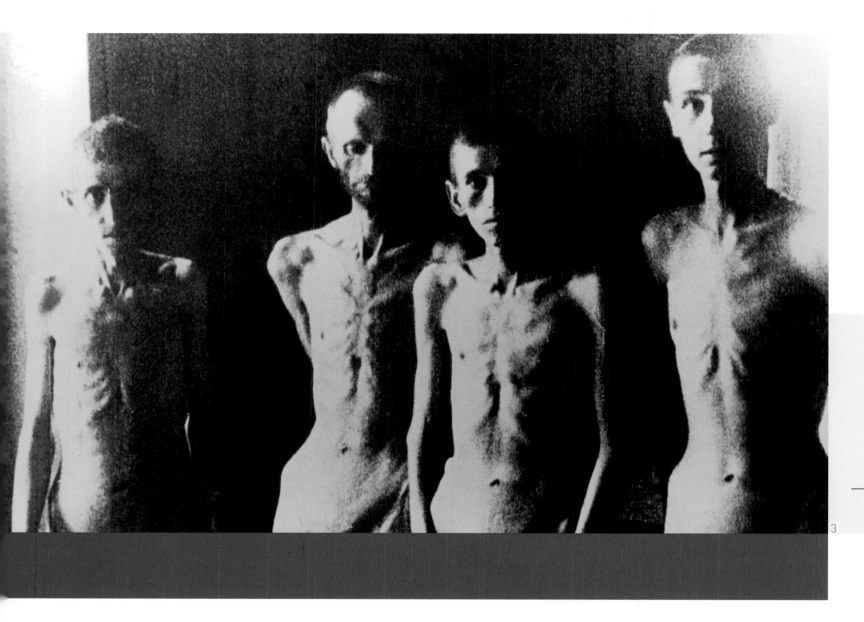

"The camp reeks of death. It is Dachau.
[...] What has happened here proves
that democratic governments, of all
persuasions, have lost sight of who
are their real leaders. They are here
in these putrid camps, where the few
survivors of a group condemned to
heroism are still struggling against
the indifference and insincerity of their
fellow men."

Camus at Combat, 17 May 1945
Reprinted in *Our Times I – Chronicles 1944–1948*,
OCII, p. 417–420

1- Nazi Germany surren-
   dered on 8 May 1945.
   The very same day, 103
   Europeans died when
   the army fired on dem-
   onstrators at Sétif and
   Guelma in north-eastern
   Algeria. Thousands of
   Algerians were killed.
   Camus was prompted to
   write a series of six arti-
   cles, parts of which were
   republished in *Algerian
   Chronicles* of 1958,
   under the title "Crisis in
   Algeria".

2- After the Sétif riots, the
   people of Algeria rallied
   and demanded inde-
   pendence. This gathering
   is at the Falaises beach
   near Kherrata.

3- Dachau survivors.

4- Local inhabitants and
   American soldiers inside
   the concentration camp
   at Dachau in 1945.

ALBERT CAMUS

LE
MALENTENDU
suivi de
CALIGULA
édition augmentée

nrf

GALLIMARD

> "Then I shall continue working on *The Misunderstanding* (that's the title of my play). It's a story about paradise lost and not regained." Letter from Albert Camus to Jean Grenier, 17 July 1943

After a twenty-year absence, a twenty-year silence, a man returns to the small Bohemian village where his mother and sister run an inn, hoping to rediscover his homeland. But he does not want to tell anyone who he is. He wants people to recognize him without having to say, "It's me!" The question is whether this is possible, whether a man's heart has a homeland, whether in fact, as he himself puts it, "he is right or wrong to imagine such things". His answer will be a simple yes or no.

This play, which is a pure tragedy, adheres to no theatrical theory. However, if there absolutely must be an idea behind it, it would be that a part of every man consists of illusions and misunderstandings and it is this part of him that must be eliminated. But it is a sacrifice that liberates another, better, part of him, which is what enables him to rebel and achieve freedom.

It is clear that this could be the subject of another play.

Programme notes to the June 1944 production of *The Misunderstanding*

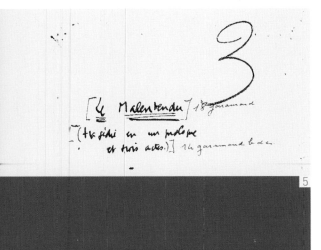

1- On 23 June 1944, Camus's *The Misunderstanding* was premiered at the Théâtre des Mathurins in Paris. The production was directed by Marcel Herrand. Peeping between the curtains at the premiere, Camus is assessing its reception. Written in 1943, *The Misunderstanding* was withdrawn after a month.

2- Camus's first two plays, *Caligula* and *The Misunderstanding*, were published by Gallimard in June 1944.

3- The character Martha was created for Maria Cesarès, who co-starred with Marcel Herrand.

4- The great tragedian Maria Cesarès met Camus in 1944. They began an affair shortly afterwards.

5- Autograph title page of 1943, marked up for typesetting.

"But the thing is, when I'm surrounded by intellectuals, I don't know why, I always feel as if I should be apologizing for something. I constantly have the impression that I've broken the rules, which of course makes me uncomfortable. And if I don't feel comfortable, I get bored." *Why I Write for the Theatre, OCIV, p. 606*

1, 2- In 1943, at the premiere of Jean-Paul Sartre's play, *Les Mouches*, Camus met the writer and his partner Simone de Beauvoir. At that meeting, Sartre asked Camus to produce his next play, *Huis clos*.

3- In 1946, Palimugre published an essay by Sartre entitled *An Explanation of The Outsider*, which was reprinted the following year as part of his *Situations I*.

4, 5- The militant couple Elsa Triolet and Louis Aragon had met Camus in Lyon, then in the unoccupied zone, in 1943. The following year, Triolet's *Who is this Outsider and Where is He From?*, which referred to Camus's *The Outsider*, was published by Seghers. Here the couple is talking to Pablo Picasso (left), who was among their friends.

6- Camus with Pierre Galindo and another friend outside the café Les Deux Magots in Paris.

7- The Café de Flore and Les Deux Magots, on the Boulevard Saint-Germain, were meeting places for Paris's intelligentsia – among them Camus.

8- Camus reading the Salvation Army paper *En Avant!* in Les Deux Magots in 1945.

In 1944, Michel and Louise Leiris organized a reading of *Catching Desire by the Tail*, a play written by Pablo Picasso and directed by Camus. The Hungarian photographer Brassaï (pseudonym of Gyula Halász) immortalized the cast – a remarkable one considering that it was improvised. From left to right: Jacques Lacan, Cécile Eluard, Pierre Reverdy, Louise Leiris, Zanie de Campan, Pablo Picasso, Valentine Hugo and Simone de Beauvoir (standing); Jean-Paul Sartre, Albert Camus, Michel Leiris and Jean Aubier (seated).

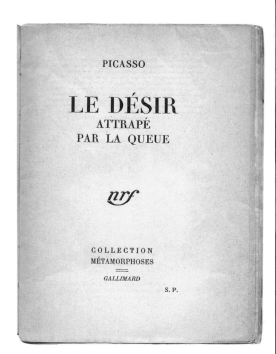

PICASSO

LE DÉSIR
ATTRAPÉ
PAR LA QUEUE

nrf

COLLECTION
MÉTAMORPHOSES
═══
GALLIMARD
                    S. P.

"With a naturalness that betrayed his familiarity with the theatre [...] he slipped in and out of the scenes conjured up by the readers, like a great actor playing Destiny who was tired of his lot."

Maria Casarès, *Privileged Resident*, Fayard, 1980

Maria Casarès is referring here to Camus, whom she met for the first time at the one and only "performance" of Picasso's *Catching Desire by the Tail*, in March 1944.

Paris, 27 January 1945

Dear Sir,

Your request has caused me a sleepless night. After due consideration I have just sent the signature you asked me for. However, your letter did nothing to move or convince me to do so.

I have signed the petition for pardon for reasons that have nothing to do with those you suggested to me, which merely helped me to find my own as I confronted the problem outlined in your letter.

I have always been disgusted by the death penalty and I decided that I could not, as a human being, condone it, even by abstention.

It is as simple as that, and no doubt Brasillach's cronies would find my squeamishness highly amusing.

As for Brasillach himself, if he is pardoned and if in two or three years' time he is granted amnesty, as is likely, I would like you to tell him this with regard to the appearance of my name on the petition.

It is not for him that I have added my signature to yours, not for either Brasillach the writer, whom I find worthless, or Brasillach the man, whom I despise unreservedly. Even if I had been tempted to think of him, the memory of two or three of my friends, mutilated and gunned down by Brasillach's cronies under the influence of his journal, would have been enough to stop me.

You say that there is an element of chance in the formation of political opinions. I cannot comment on that, but I do know that there is no question of chance in the decision to act dishonourably.

Nor is it by chance that my signature appears alongside yours whereas Brasillach never used his pen in support of [Georges] Politzer or Jacques Decour.

This, therefore, is what I would like you to tell Brasillach, but also that I am not a hateful person and am more inclined towards anonymity than politics.

Maybe that will help him to grasp the nuances of my message that might have escaped him and to understand why I could never bring myself to shake his hand.

Letter from Albert Camus to Marcel Aymé, OCII, p. 733

"I have always been disgusted by the death penalty and I decided that I could not, as a human being, condone it, even by abstention."

Letter from Albert Camus to Marcel Aymé, OCII, p. 733

1- By 1944, Camus was a well-known columnist and writer. These snapshots (right and previous pages), taken by Henri Cartier-Bresson, who was to found the Magnum photographic agency in 1947, were published worldwide.

2- The trial of Marshal Pétain in August 1945. Camus can be seen in the audience.

"You say that there is an element of chance in the formation of political opinions. I cannot comment on that, but I do know that there is no question of chance in the decision to act dishonourably." Letter from Albert Camus to Marcel Aymé, OCII, p. 733

2

But I just wanted to prevent any misunderstanding. When the writer of these letters says "you", he does not mean "you Germans", but "you Nazis". And when he says "we", that does not always mean "we French" but rather "we free Europeans". I am contrasting two attitudes, not two nations, even though, at a particular historical moment, those nations came to represent hostile attitudes.

Letters to a German Friend, OCII, p. 7

I am writing to you on the eve of your defeat, from a world-famous city which is preparing to free itself from your grasp. The city knows that this will not be easy and that it must first endure a night darker even than that of four years ago, the night that marked your arrival. I am writing to you from a city in the grip of deprivation, without fuel or light, without food, but still not subdued. Soon it will breathe again, as you have never seen it breathe. If we are lucky, we will then come face to face. We will then be able to settle our differences out in the open: I have a fair idea of your reasons and you can doubtless imagine mine.

These July nights are at once light and heavy. Light where it falls on the Seine and the trees but heavy on the hearts of those who are waiting for the only dawn they now long for. I too am waiting, and I am thinking of you, for I have one more thing to tell you, which will be the last. I want to tell you how it was possible for us to be so alike and yet to become enemies, how we could so easily have stood side by side and why we shall never again be able to do so.

For a long time, we both believed that the world was subject to no higher order and that we must learn to live with that frustration. In a way, I still believe this. But I have drawn different conclusions from that belief than those which you have been telling me about and which you have been trying for several years to impose upon History. I realize now that if I had followed you in your reasoning, I would today have to approve of what you have done. And that realization has such terrible implications that I must stop thinking about it and think only of this summer night heavy with promise for us and so heavy with foreboding for you.

Letters to a German Friend, OCII, p. 25

1

"I am shocked and horrified by your news. It has been haunting me ever since I received it and I can think of nothing else. My greatest regret now is not to have told him how much I loved him, how precious his existence was to me. But men don't say such things. They wait until they are dying, and then it's too late."

Letter from Albert Camus to Ellen Leynaud, 1944

"I hate only killers. Anyone reading my *Letters to a German Friend* with this in mind, in other words as a document supporting the campaign against violence, must admit that I can now say I stand by every word."

Letters to a German Friend, Preface, OCII, p. 7

"Nothing could dissuade him once he had decided what was right. It took a belt full of bullets to bring him down."

Foreword to *Posthumous Poems* by René Leynaud, OCII, p. 706

"Another thing to take into account is the temptation to succumb to hatred. Watching people you love being shot is not a good way to learn compassion. It is a temptation that must be resisted. I did so, and it was a valuable experience." *Tomorrow is Today's Challenge*, interview by Jean Bloch-Michel, 24–30 October 1957, OCIV, p. 585

2

3

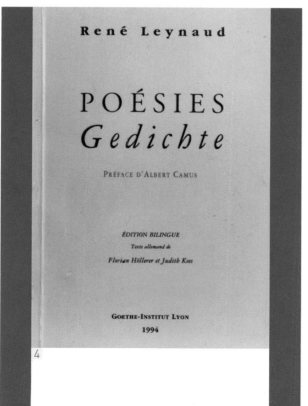

4

"He loved truth and life and everything that is worthy in the world."
Foreword to *Posthumous Poems* by René Leynaud, OCII, p. 705

"Truth needs witnesses and Leynaud was one. That is why I miss him so much."
Foreword to *Posthumous Poems* by René Leynaud, OCII, p. 711

1- In 1945, while staying with Guy Schoeller at Bougival, near Paris, Camus published a series of four letters under the title *Letters to a German Friend*. The *Letters* were dedicated to his late friend and fellow resistance fighter René Leynaud, who had been shot in 1944, and represent a train of thought that goes beyond hatred.

2, 3- René Leynaud, whose poems were published by Gallimard in 1947, with a Foreword by Camus.

4- A 1994 bilingual edition of Leynaud's poems.

1

2

"We may sum up in two sentences. Human technology has just reached new depths of murderousness. Sooner or later, we must choose between collective suicide and the intelligent use of scientific invention."

Camus at Combat, 8 August 1945. Reprinted in *Our Times I – Chronicles 1944–1948*, OCII, p. 409

"We are in fact being told, with great excitement, that any medium-sized town can be obliterated by a bomb the size of a football."

Camus at Combat, 8 August 1945. Reprinted in *Our Times I – Chronicles 1944–1948*, OCII, p. 409

1- The mushroom cloud over the Japanese city of Hiroshima.

2- Corpses amid the apocalyptic scene at Nagasaki after the explosion of the second atomic bomb.

3- For Camus, 6 August 1945 was a date that marked a critical moment in human history: the dropping of an atomic bomb on Hiroshima by the United States of America. A second bomb destroyed Nagasaki three days later. Camus spoke of "the terrifying perspectives that have opened before humanity".

3

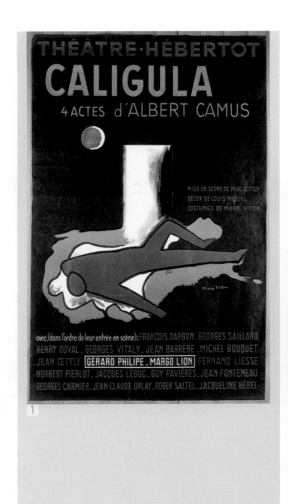

1- Poster for *Caligula*,
 whose premiere took
 place on 26 September
 1945 at the Théâtre
 Hébertot in Paris.

2- Camus with Jacques
 Hébertot and Paul Oettly.

3- Gérard Philipe, who
 played the title role in
 Caligula.

4- Michel Bouquet and
 Gérard Philipe in *Cali-
 gula*. The costumes were
 designed by Marie Viton.

5- A rehearsal for *Caligula*.

"I have discovered a very simple truth: men die unhappy." *Caligula*, OCI, p. 322

"Caligula (*collapsing onto his bed with a satisfied and spontaneous laugh*): No, but just look at them, Caesonia. They've abandoned everything. Honesty and respectability, what do they mean? National pride? Nothing means anything any more. Fear banishes all other feelings. Fear, my dear Caesonia, that admirable sentiment, unalloyed, pure and selfless, one of the rare feelings whose nobility comes straight from the stomach. (*He wipes his brow with his hand and drinks. In a friendly tone.*) Let us change the subject now. But Cherea, you seem to have lost your tongue."

Caligula, Act II, Scene V, OCI, p. 347

"We've just had a girl and a boy in one go."

Letter from Albert Camus to Nicola Chiaromonte, 5 October 1945

1- Handwritten letter from Camus to Nicola Chiaromonte dated 5 October 1945.

2 to 5- After the liberation of France, Francine, who had been living and working as a teacher in Oran since October 1942, was at last able to contemplate making the journey to Paris to rejoin her husband. She arrived in September 1944 after a roundabout sea voyage via the Bay of Biscay. On 5 September the following year, Francine gave birth to twins, Catherine and Jean. The babies arrived in the middle of rehearsals for Caligula, just three weeks before the premiere at the Théâtre Hébertot.

6- Camus at the home of Guy Schoeller in Bougival in November 1945.

1, 2, 3- Francine and Albert with
          their twins at Bougival in
          November 1945.

    4- Camus reacquaint-
        ing himself with the
        Mediterranean on the
        Ile Saint-Honorat off
        Cannes in 1945.

THE CENTURY OF FEAR

Indeed, a climate of fear is not one that encourages reflection. However, it is my belief that, instead of using that fear as an excuse, we should recognize it as one of the prime causes of the current situation and try to find a remedy for it. This is of paramount importance, since it would affect the lives of so many Europeans. They have had enough of violence and deceit, their greatest hopes have been crushed and they are repulsed by the thought of killing their neighbours, even if they are told that this is necessary in order to convince them of the truth, but they are equally repulsed by the idea that they themselves might be subjected to the same treatment. Yet this is the dilemma in which the vast majority of Europeans find themselves – people who belong to no political party, or who are unhappy with the one they do belong to, who do not believe that socialism is working in Russia, or liberalism in America, but who do believe that, wherever they live, people have the right to say what they think yet no right to impose their ideas by murdering others, either individually or collectively. These are today's powerless, the rulers of nothing.

Neither Victims nor Executioners, The Century of Fear, OCII, p. 437

Rebellion. 1946–1951

"What is a rebel? Someone who says no. But saying no does not mean giving up: it also means saying yes, with every gesture."

Man as Rebel, OCIII, p. 71

"We enter New York Harbor. An impressive sight despite, or perhaps because of, the mist. It is a show of strength, order and economic power."

Notebooks 1935–1948, OCII, p. 1052

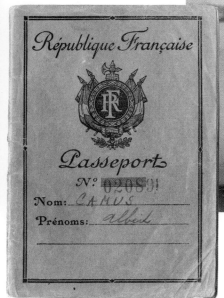

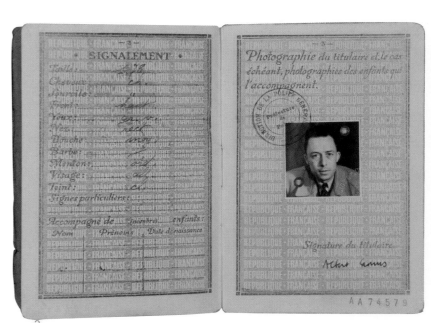

New York rain is alienating. Heavy, oily and dense, it pours tirelessly between the towering blocks of cement onto the suddenly pitch-dark avenues. Having taken refuge in a taxi halted by red lights and propelled onwards by green lights, I feel trapped, mesmerized by the monotonous thrashing of the windscreen wipers as they fight to clear the flood of water. I am sure that we could drive for hours without ever getting free of the prison blocks we are wading amongst, with no hope of seeing so much as a hill or a tree. Seemingly destabilized by the grey mist, the bleached skyscrapers loom like gigantic tombs in this city of the dead. I therefore abandon myself to time. Eight million people amid the smell of iron and cement, construction gone mad, solitude at its height. "Were I to gather around me every living human being, yet would I be defenceless."

Rain in New York, OCII, p. 690

"[...] New York has got into me like a foreign body into my eye – at once unbearable and delectable. It makes me cry pitifully and fly into a blind rage. Perhaps that is what is called passion."

Rain in New York, OCII, p. 690

"Yes, I am out of my depth. I have discovered that there are cities that are like certain women, who stun you and scorch your soul, whose intensity scars your whole body, at once shockingly and delectably."

Rain in New York, OCII, p. 692

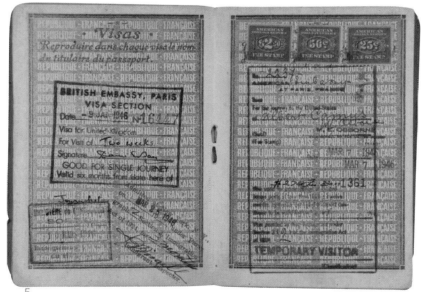

4

5

1, 3, 5– Camus's passport. In 1946, he was invited to give a series of lectures on the other side of the Atlantic.

2– 10 March 1946: Camus leaves Le Havre aboard the *Oregon*, a simple freighter, bound for New York.

4– Manhattan Island, New York in about 1945.

1- Broadway at night.

2- In New York Camus met Hachette representative Jacques Shoeller.

3- A street in Harlem.

4- List of items Camus brought back to France, where there were still shortages, after two months in New York.

5- Camus visited Canada before returning home.

Perhaps it is because New York is nothing without its sky. Stretched out to the four corners of the horizon like a blank canvas, it gives the city its morning glory and its evening splendour, the burning sun setting over 8th Avenue, where the crowds flow between the shop windows, lit up well before dark. And, occasionally, as the dusk reddens the water along Riverside, where the freeway runs alongside the Hudson into the city, the soft, well oiled rumble from the continuous stream of cars suddenly sounds like the gentle swishing of waves. [...] But when the sky is dull or when the day is over, New York becomes the big city once again – prison by day, funeral pyre by night.

Rain in New York, OCII, p. 690

"I love New York, with the kind of passion that can leave you full of uncertainty and repugnance: sometimes we need to be exiled."

Rain in New York, OCII, p. 693

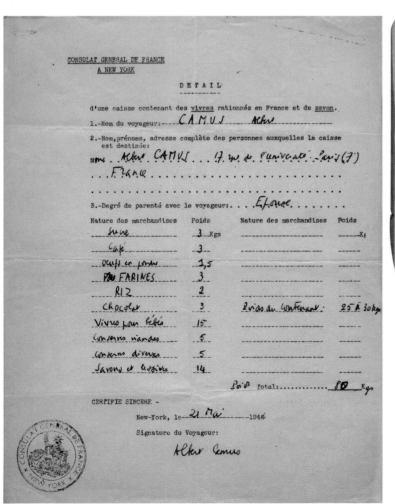

2

3

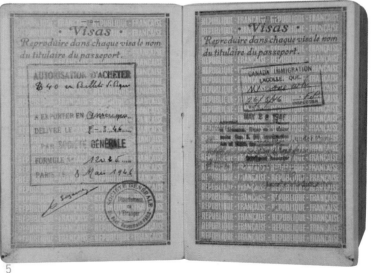

5

4

"Quebec's magnificent landscapes. At the tip of Cape Diamond, where cliffs plunge to the St Lawrence, air, light and water blur into infinity. For the first time on this continent a real sensation of beauty and grandeur."

Notebooks 1935–1948, OCII, p. 1061

1 to 4- In August 1946, Camus spends time with Francine at Les Brefs, the home of Michel Gallimard in the Vendée, and works on *The Plague*.

5, 6, 8- Albert and Francine with the twins.

7- Camus dedicated his translation of James Thurber's *The Last Flower* to his children "in the fervent hope that their world will be better than mine".

Catherine et Jean

POUR ~~ROSEMARY~~,
leur
AVEC L'ESPOIR ARDENT QUE ~~BON~~ MONDE
SERA MEILLEUR QUE LE MIEN.

7

8

"Time doesn't go quickly when we're looking at it. It senses that it's being watched. But it takes advantage of moments when we're concentrating on something else. Perhaps, in fact, there are two types of time: the one we keep an eye on and the one that changes us."

Notebooks 1935–1948, OCII, p. 995

"At the age of thirty, virtually overnight, I became famous. I don't regret it. Had it happened later, it might have given me sleepless nights. Now I know what fame is. Nothing much."

Notebooks 1935–1948, OCII, p. 1033

1- Camus with Michel Gallimard and his daughter Anne.

2- Camus met Michel Gallimard in 1942 when *The Outsider* was published. Like Camus, Gallimard had tuberculosis and understood the value of life. The two were to become close friends.

3- Camus is given a lift by Pierre and Michel Gallimard.

4- Camus with Michel and Janine Gallimard in Grasse.

5- Camus in the garden at the Gallimards' with Jean Paulhan and Marcel Arland, who became Director and Co-director, respectively, of *La Nouvelle Revue Française* in 1953.

5

1- In 1946, Camus became acquainted with Louis Guilloux, who, two years later, invited him to Algeria for a writers' workshop in Sidi-Madani near Blida. In 1953, when Guilloux produced a new edition of his *House of the People*, he included as a foreword a 1948 article on democracy Camus had written for the magazine *Caliban*.

2- Camus relaxes at Pornic in Brittany in 1946.

3- Camus with the poet René Char in his native village, L'Isle-sur-la-Sorgue in Provence, where he later bought a property. It was here, well away from Paris, that Camus finished *The Plague*.

4- Handwritten letter from Camus to René Char dated 1946: "In the short time he is allotted, he stimulates and illuminates, without deviating from his mortal trajectory. Sown by the wind and harvested by the wind, he is at once transitory seed and universal creator. Such is man across the centuries, proud to live but for an instant!"

5- In October 1945, Camus was appointed editor of Gallimard's *Collection Espoir* series, as part of which he published René Char's *Hypnos Album*.

6- *After the Sun*, a collection of poetical texts and photographs that was the fruit of Camus's deep friendship with René Char, was published posthumously.

Books and magazines written by specialists in social evolution talk about the proletariat as if it were a cult with weird practices, in a way that would revolt proletarians themselves – if only they had time to read specialist books and magazines to learn how they should be evolving. It is hard to say which aspect of their sermons is more insulting: their fulsome flattery or their naive mockery. [...] Fortunately, a few men [...] have found the appropriate tone, and it is for this that I admire and appreciate the work of Louis Guilloux, who neither flatters nor mocks the people he is writing about but who restores their intrinsic nobility by speaking the truth.

Foreword to *House of the People* by Louis Guilloux, OCII, p. 712

"Guilloux: 'In fact, writers do not write in order to say things, but in order not to have to say them.'"
Notebooks 1949–1959, OCIV, p. 1067

"Char is the greatest thing that has happened to French poetry since Rimbaud."

Interview for *Diario*, São Paulo, 1949, OCIII, p. 867

A René Char

Dans le jour bref qui lui est donné, il réchauffe et illumine, sans dévier de sa course mortelle. Semé par le vent, moissonné par le vent, graine éphémère et cependant soleil créateur, tel est l'homme, à travers les siècles, fier de vivre un seul instant !

"To tell the truth, I was sad when you left. Meeting certain people brings greater rewards than one normally has in a month of Sundays."
Letter from René Char to Albert Camus, 4 October 1947

"[...] he [Char] makes something new and fresh of the tough, sparse tradition of southern thought. He was born into the harsh, bare light of Provence. And it is deeply significant that his healing words come to us from that country, at once soft and aloof, where the evenings are mournful and agonizing, the mornings as pristine as a new world, and which, like all other Mediterranean countries, patiently preserves the springs of life from which one day, exhausted and ashamed, Europe will drink and find renewal."
Curtain up on ... René Char, OCII, p. 765

"*After the Sun* was the product of my meeting with a young photographer named Henriette Grindat, Camus's increasing delight in discovering my part of France, and my own feelings [...]"
René Char, *Birth and Growth of a Friendship*, *After the Sun*, OCIV, p. 735

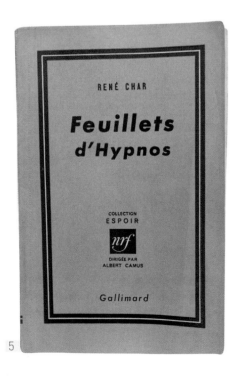

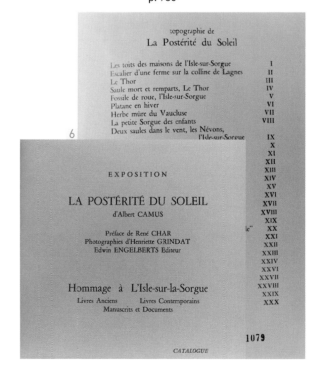

"Later, after the liberation of France, I received a letter from Camus asking me if he could include my *Hypnos Album*, whose manuscript I had sent to Gallimard some weeks earlier, in their *Collection Espoir*. I was unaware of this series, which Camus was launching with a number of works that he had selected personally. I was attracted by his proposal and agreed. I had read one or two of his articles in *Combat* and admired their clarity and integrity. That was all I knew about him."
After the Sun, Afterword by Rene Char, OCIV, p. 733
Correspondence 1946–1959, Gallimard, 2007, p. 21

1- *The Plague* was published in 1947. An allegorical novel about oppression in all its forms, it was immediately successful. However, in 1946, Camus had written in his *Notebooks*: "Plague. Never in my life have I had such a sense of failure. I'm not even sure if I'll be able to finish it. Sometimes, though…"

2- *The Plague Archives*, a collection of sketches and drafts for the novel, was also published in 1947 as the second of La Pléiade's *Notebooks*.

3, 4- Having won the Critics' Prize in 1947, Camus was interviewed and entertained by journalists.

5- Camus in 1947. He was 34.

6- Jules Roy, Gabriel Audisio, Janine Montupet and Albert Camus, all North African writers, at a book signing.

"Lots of people in our town started philosophizing and went around saying that it was no good doing anything, people must simply bow to the inevitable. Tarrou and Rieux and the others would say this or that but they already knew what had to be done: one way or another they had to fight, they could not simply bow to the inevitable. The only thing that mattered was to prevent as many people as possible from dying and from losing their loved ones. And there was only one way of doing that, which was to fight against the plague."

The Plague, OCII, p. 125

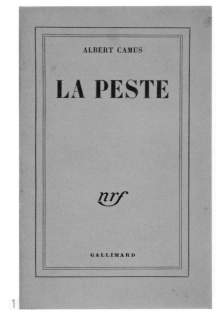

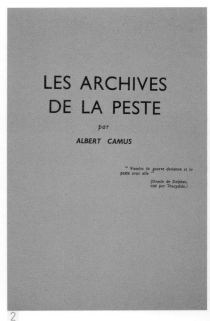

"It is a very great book, and it will grow in stature."

Louis Guilloux to Albert Camus, cited in *Albert Camus, A Life* by Olivier Todd, Gallimard, 1996, p. 481

"[...] every one of us is a carrier because no one, and I mean no one in the world, is immune to the plague. And we must constantly be on the look-out so that we don't inadvertently breathe on anyone and contaminate them."

The Plague, OCII, p. 209

"The only thing that is natural is the virus itself. Everything else – health, integrity, purity, if you like – is the result of willpower, a willpower that must be constantly maintained. The honest ones, those who contaminate the fewest people, are the ones who don't let themselves be distracted."

The Plague, OCII, p. 209

"To René Char, 'It only remains...', in memory of times of *Plague*, which brought us together, as they should. With my admiration and brotherly love, Albert Camus."

Camus's dedication on the copy of *The Plague* he gave to René Char, 1947

"My dear Camus,

I regret that I do not have the energy to tell you all the great things I found in *The Plague*. This beautiful book made me understand better still why I am your devoted friend."

Letter from André Gide to Albert Camus, 16 June 1947

1 to 3- After the success of *The Plague*, Camus took a break with Francine and the twins at Le Panelier, a small hotel up in the hills near Saint-Étienne run by the mother of the director Paul Oettly. Camus had stayed there several times in 1942, while he was writing *The Misunderstanding*, and again the following year. The clean air was good for his health.

4 to 6- Camus and Francine relax with their children, Catherine and Jean.

"Le Panelier, 17 June 1947. Wonderful day. The light sparkles and dances softly on and around the giant beeches, as if secreted from its very branches." *Notebooks 1935–1948*, OCII, p. 1083

4

5

6

1- Camus with his daughter, Catherine.
2- Francine with the twins, aged 18 months.
3- Francine at Le Panelier, summer 1947.

"But no sooner were the walls covered with pictures than the rooms were full of children and they had to think of a different way of using the space. Before the arrival of their third child, Jonas had worked in the main room and Louise had done her knitting in their bedroom, while the two little ones shared the second bedroom, throwing themselves about and running around the rest of the apartment whenever they had a chance."

Exile and the Kingdom, Jonas or the Artist at Work, OCIV, p. 65

1- The action of *State of Siege* takes place in Spain, during Franco's dictatorship. Otherwise, it is based on the same theme as *The Plague*. The premiere, at the Théâtre Marigny, was on 27 October 1948. It was not a box office hit.

2, 5- Camus with Jean-Louis Barrault, who directed the production. The set and costume designs were by Balthus and the music by Arthur Honegger.

3- Jean-Pierre Granval and Jean Desailly (front).

4- Camus with Jean-Louis Barrault and his wife, Madeleine Renaud, who had left the Comédie-Française in 1946 to found the Renaud-Barrault theatre company with her husband. Among the plays they staged was *State of Siege*.

"At its first performance in Paris, the critics reacted as one to *State of Siege*. Indeed, few plays can have received such a unanimous lambasting. It is all the more regrettable because I have always thought that *State of Siege*, despite its many faults, is possibly the work that is most like me."
Foreword to the American edition, 1958; *State of Siege*, Appendices, OCII, p. 372

"The Plague: The fact is, I am the ruler here and so I have the right to rule, and no one else has a right to say otherwise. Get used to the idea. [...] Fisherman: O sea, thy billows are rebellious, thy people shall never submit."

State of Siege, OCII, p. 322 and p. 366

"He who lives in hope does not love life."

Back and Front, Foreword, OCI, p. 36

1- Camus at a flea market
   in 1953.
2- Madeleine Renaud as
   Secretary to The Plague,
   Jean-Louis Barrault,
   who also directed,
   as Diego, and Maria
   Casarès as Victoria in
   the first production of
   State of Siege.
3- Camus's own introduc-
   tion to the programme
   for *State of Siege* printed
   for the premiere at the
   Théâtre Marigny.
4, 6- Théâtre Marigny programme cover and cast
   list.
5- Pierre Brasseur and
   Maria Casarès, who had
   previously acted together
   in Marcel Carné's classic
   film *Children of Paradise.*

1

2

AVANT-PROPOS

En 1941, Barrault eut l'idée de monter un spectacle autour du thème de la peste, qui avait tenté aussi Antonin Artaud. Dans les années qui suivirent, il lui parut plus simple d'adapter à cet effet le grand livre de Daniel de Foe, " *Le Journal de la Peste* ". Il fit alors le canevas d'une mise en scène.

Lorsqu'il sut que, de mon coté, j'allais publier un roman sur le même thème, il m'offrit d'écrire des dialogues sur ce canevas. J'avais d'autres idées sur la question et, en particulier, il me paraissait préférable d'oublier Daniel de Foe et de revenir à la première idée de Barrault. Nos premières conversations nous amenèrent donc à imaginer une sorte de mythe moderne. Ce que ce projet est devenu après plus d'un an de travail ininterrompu, dans la collaboration la plus étroite, on le verra. Quant à ce qu'il vaut, ce n'est pas à moi de le dire.

Mais, 1°) il doit être clair que " l'État de Siège " quoiqu'on en ait dit, n'est à aucun degré une adaptation de mon roman.

2°) Il ne s'agit pas d'une pièce de structure traditionnelle, mais d'un spectacle dont l'ambition avouée est de mêler toutes les formes d'expression dramatique depuis le monologue lyrique jusqu'au théâtre collectif en passant par le jeu muet, le simple dialogue, la farce et le chœur.

3°) S'il est vrai que j'ai écrit tout le texte, il reste que le nom de Barrault devrait, en toute justice, être réuni au mien. Et si

Barrault s'y est refusé pour des raisons que je respecte, il me revient au moins de dire ici ce que " l'État de Siège " lui doit.

Pour le reste, on verra suffisamment qu'il s'agit d'une pièce de colère, mais sur ce sujet je n'aurai qu'un mot à ajouter : j'avais pensé à appeler ce spectacle : " l'Amour de Vivre ".

3

4

5

6

"Why Spain? Because we are the few who refuse to wash our hands in these people's blood." *Combat*, "Why Spain?", December 1948, OCII, p. 484

Reprinted in *Our Times I – Chronicles 1944–1948*, OCII, p. 484

"I cannot excuse this hideous plague that is infesting western Europe because its ravages are also being felt in the east, on an even vaster scale."
Combat, "Why Spain?", December 1948, OCII, p. 484
Reprinted in *Our Times I – Chronicles 1944–1948*, OCII, p. 485

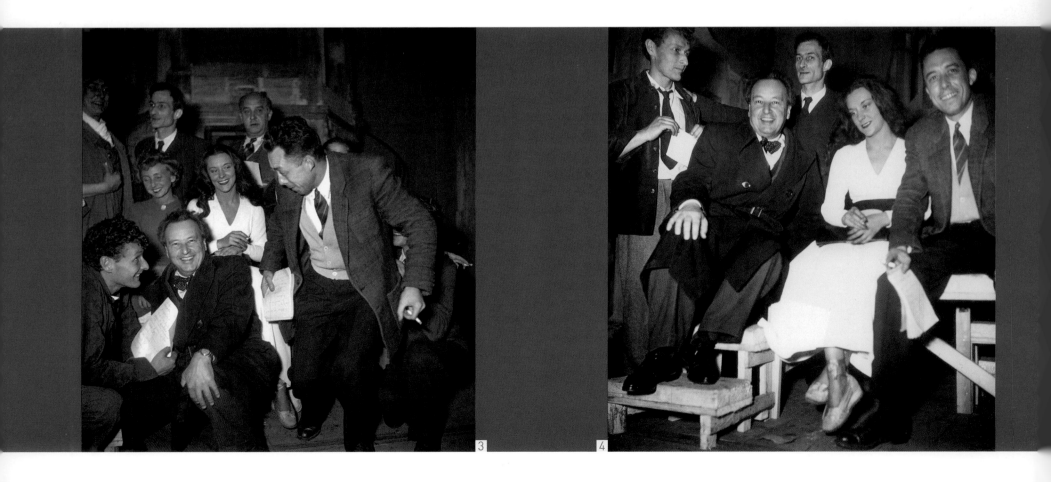

"Janine did not know why this idea filled her with such sweet and profound sadness that she had to shut her eyes. She knew only that, for as long as she could remember, she had been promised this kingdom but that it would never be hers, except perhaps in the fleeting moment when, opening her eyes again, she would see the flood of lights, unblinking in the motionless sky. [...] Wherever she was, from now on, life would be suspended, except in her heart, where, at that very moment, someone was crying in pain and amazement."
Exile and the Kingdom, The Adulterous Woman, OCIV, p. 14

1- Camus with Jean-Louis Barrault and Arthur Honegger.

2- Camus with Balthus, Pierre Brasseur, Gabriel Cattand, Jean-Louis Barrault and an unnamed other during a rehearsal for *State of Siege* at the Théâtre Marigny.

3- At the Théâtre Marigny: Jean-Louis Barrault, Arthur Honegger and Albert Camus (front); Madeleine Renaud and Maria Casarès (middle); Pierre Brasseur, Balthus and Gabriel Cattand (back).

4- Arthur Honegger, Maria Casarès and Albert Camus (seated); Jean-Louis Barrault and Balthus (standing).

5- Francine with Madeleine Renaud at the premiere of *State of Siege* on 27 October 1948.

We didn't get to Buenos Aires until midday. Lack of sleep is weighing me down at the moment. V. O. came to meet me but no one from the embassy, and they hadn't got me a ticket for Montevideo, where I had to speak at 6.30 p.m. Thanks to V., we went straight to Buenos Aires and on to the hydroplane port. They were all full. V. phoned a friend and fixed everything. We take off at 4.45 through a yellow fog over a yellow sea. At 5.45 we land in Montevideo. This time the embassy has sent someone, but he informs me that they decided to cancel the conference and take me to the French school instead. There, the headmaster tells me that there are some people who want to hear me all the same and he doesn't know what to do. I suggest holding a discussion, even though I'm washed out. They agree and my two lectures are rescheduled for the following day, the first at 11 a.m., the second at 6 p.m. I go straight to bed after the discussion, dead on my feet.

Draft of a letter to Pierre Bergé, *Notebooks 1949–1959*, OCIV, p. 1052

16 July 1949 ... When I arrive at Mrs M's, everyone is in a state of anxiety. The Saintly Father (the priest, who is also the principal dancer), who is supposed to have organized the *macumba*, asked permission of the relevant saint but was refused. Abdias, the black actor, is reproaching himself more than anyone for not offering enough money to ensure the saint's goodwill. He suggests taking a trip to Caxias, [...] twenty-five miles from Rio, where we might see a *macumba*. These ceremonies all seem to have the same aim: to let god enter the body by dancing and singing. The idea is to get into a trance. What distinguishes the *macumba* from other similar ceremonies is its mixture of Catholic sacrament and African ritual. In the way of gods and saints there are Echou, the African god of evil, and Ogoun, who is like our Saint George. There's also Saint Cosme and Saint Damien and others. This worship of saints is tied up with rites of possession. There is a saint for each day and you may not worship any other saint on that day without special permission from the "Saintly Father". The Saintly Father is responsible for ensuring that his daughters (and, presumably, sons) get themselves into the right sort of trance.

Notebooks 1949–1959, OCIV, p. 1022

A Macumba in Brazil, previously unpublished extract from a travel diary, dated 16 July 1949. This entry would be the basis of a passage in *The Stone that Grew*, one of the essays that make up *Exile and the Kingdom*, OCIV, p. 80

1

"I love the night sky more than men's gods."
Notebooks 1949–1959, OCIV, p. 1027

2

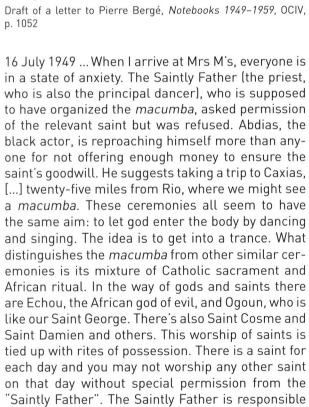

1- In July 1949, Camus crossed the Atlantic for a second time to give a series of lectures in South America. Travelling from Argentina to Chile, the writer covered thousands of miles. Here he is in Rio de Janeiro, in front of the Christ the Redeemer statue on Mount Corcovado.

2- Camus with some admirers.

3- Press coverage of Camus's South American lectures.

4- Rio de Janeiro in the 1950s.

Translation of newspaper article headlines.

"Camus the Activist. 'In this age of despotism, tyranny and dictatorship, we creative artists must defend our greatest value: freedom.'"
24 August 1949

[Note to Editor: Quotes within quotes added, as in original.]

"Freedom is without doubt the great challenge of our age. Towards a new classicism – The century of tyranny – The duty of the creative artist – Mr Camus speaks"
16 August 1949

"'I neither am nor ever will be an existentialist,' said the French philosopher Albert Camus yesterday"
16 August 1949

"A message from Albert Camus"
21 August 1949

"Camus, absurdist writer, says: 'I am not an existentialist; the 20th century is the century of despotism; the last revolution was Freud's'"
23 August 1949

"With its flimsy modern armour plating stretched over an immense continent pulsating with primitive natural forces, Brazil reminds me of a tower block whose facade is gradually being eaten away by invisible termites. One day the tower will collapse and the little pulsating creatures, black, red and yellow, will swarm all over the surface of the continent, wearing masks and brandishing spears as they dance in celebration of victory."
Notebooks 1949–1959, OCIV, p. 1036

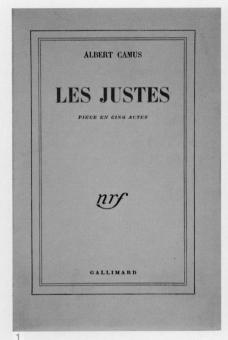

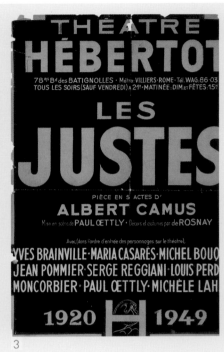

1

2

3

1- *The Just*, a play in five acts. In it, Camus evokes the 1905 plot to assassinate the Grand Duke of Russia. It was published by Gallimard in 1950.

2- Camus acquired photographs of 14 of the men involved in the plot, including this one, of Ivan Kaliayev. On it Camus has written "Kaliayev after his arrest".

3- Poster for *The Just*, which was premiered at the Théâtre Hébertot on 15 December 1949. The production was directed by Paul Oettly.

4- Serge Reggiani and Maria Casarès played the principal parts of Kaliayev and Dora, whose raison d'être is rebellion and whose motivation is the desire for justice and innocence.

5- Typescript page from *The Just* with annotations by the author.

6- Camus with Maria Casarès.

4

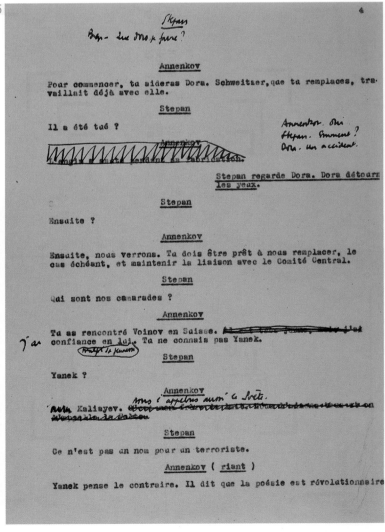

5

"But when I looked at his face, a face that I had known for so long [...]" Maria Casarès, *Privileged Resident*, Fayard, 1980, p. 239

6

"Later, I thought a lot about the problem of writing a modern tragedy. *The Misunderstanding*, *State of Siege* and *The Just* are attempts, each one in a different way and a different style, to find a way of writing a modern tragedy."
Interview for *Paris-Théâtre*, OCIV, p. 578

Looking into his eyes, penetrating, clairvoyant, frank, merci-
lessly searching but always compassionate; listening to his
voice, confiding and passionate, painfully vehement, proud,
ironic, friendly, and to his vivid recollections, which never so-
licit attention but merely recount, and in doing so show respect
and deference for his listeners; hearing his indefatigable ap-
peal to man and god, his cry of NO to injustice, deceit, suffering
and death, and to every injunction, whatever its pretext, that
results in men being subjugated or forced to abandon their
one great adventure, the adventure of the spirit; and seeing
the struggle he imposed upon himself against lethargy, un-
justified anger, indifference, avoidance, pride and weakness of
every other kind; in short, in the face of the contradictions that
humans must face and come to terms with in order to become
human beings, I suddenly realized how many contradictions
there were in me and, at the same time, that here in front of me
was the opportunity for the greatest joy and for the cruellest
and most intense pain.

Maria Casarès, *Privileged Resident*, Fayard, 1980, p. 239

[...] I think of him [...] so curious about everything, so open to
everything, so unique in everything, so outside everything, like
a tree that has been uprooted and buried but forces its roots
to the other side of the earth in order to find or to rediscover
fresh air to breathe with all those who, like him, are stifling
– simultaneously defending himself and making himself vul-
nerable; I think of him torn between an understanding of the
world and an understanding of men, allowing himself no room
for dreams but keeping the thread of his existence taught from
one day to the next, keeping to the narrow path he had to follow in order to maintain his pact of solidarity with those he
acknowledged as being worthy of living according to the only
order he could accept, that of honesty and truthfulness – Prometheus choosing Sisyphus's fate and burning Icarus's wings.

Maria Casarès, *Privileged Resident*, Fayard, 1980, p. 240

"The theatre gives me the sense of
camaraderie and collective adventure
that I need and that is still among the
most rewarding ways of being with
other people."
Interview on *France Soir*, 1958, OCIV, p. 651

1

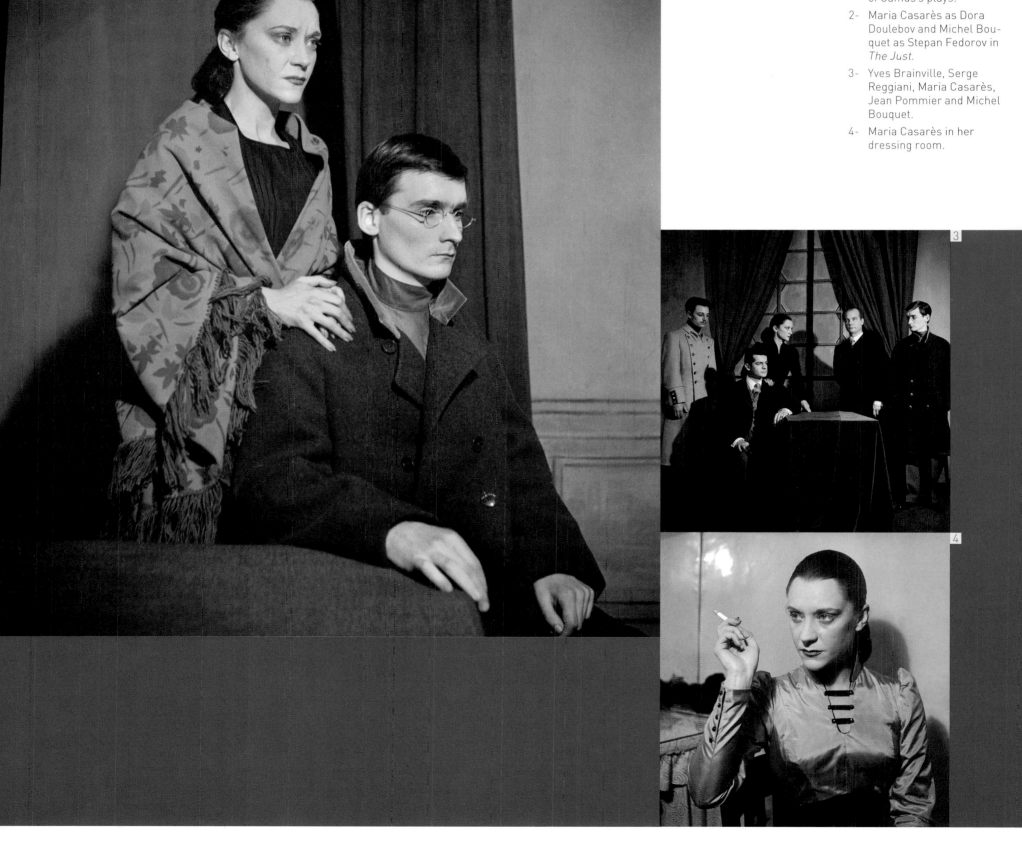

1- Camus with Maria
Casarès and Serge Reg-
giani in the wings of the
Théâtre Hébertot. The
role of Dora was her third
in premiere productions
of Camus's plays.

2- Maria Casarès as Dora
Doulebov and Michel Bou-
quet as Stepan Fedorov in
The Just.

3- Yves Brainville, Serge
Reggiani, Maria Casarès,
Jean Pommier and Michel
Bouquet.

4- Maria Casarès in her
dressing room.

For years, I saw in the death penalty only unimaginable suffering and arbitrary indifference, neither of which my sense of reason could accept. I was nevertheless ready to accept that my imagination was colouring my judgement. But in fact, during those weeks, I found nothing to support that hypothesis or to modify my attitude. On the contrary, I found that others had the same attitude as I did. Today, I share Koestler's conviction: that the death penalty is a stain on our society and that its supporters can find no logical justification for it. Without repeating his argument or listing facts and figures that would add nothing to it – and that are unnecessary in view of Jean Bloch-Michel's detailed account – I shall simply pursue a line of reasoning that extrapolates Koestler's own thinking and, like the latter, argues for the immediate abolition of capital punishment.

Reflections on the Guillotine, OCIV, p. 130

"[...] it is difficult to see how it [the death penalty] should, as it was supposed to, bring peace and order to inner cities. On the contrary, it seems all too obvious that it is no less revolting than the murders it is intended to compensate for, and that this additional crime, far from repairing the damage done to the social fabric, merely adds another layer of filth to it. It is so obvious, in fact, that no one dares to talk openly about these ceremonial killings." *Reflections on the Guillotine*, OCIV, p. 128

Arthur Koestler / Albert Camus
Réflexions sur la peine capitale

1, 4- Albert and Francine Camus in England.

2- In 1957, Calmann-Lévy published two essays under the title *Reflections on Capital Punishment*: Arthur Koestler's *Reflections on Hanging* and Camus's *Reflections on the Guillotine*. The two essays were to reappear in 2002 under Gallimard's *Folio* imprint.

3- Arthur Koestler.

1, 2– Francine and Albert Camus in 1952, at the window of their apartment in Rue Madame, Paris, which they had bought two years earlier with money from the sale of *The Plague*.

"Novel. The stone lovers. And he now knew what had caused him so much suffering throughout this relationship and why it could not have been prevented unless ... at the critical moment ... some kind of zephyr had petrified them in the very act of falling in love and they had from then on stood like statues facing one another, freed from the world's cruel grip, knowing nothing of the desires that whirled furiously about them but each turned to face the other as if towards the perfect image of mutual love."
Notebooks 1949–1959, OCIV, p. 1006

2

"People continue to confuse love and marriage on the one hand and love and happiness on the other. Yet they have nothing in common. That is why, given that the absence of love is more prevalent than the presence of love, marriages are often happy." *Notebooks 1949–1959*, OCIV, p. 1066

At Le Panelier in 1950. From left to right: Jean, Francine, Manette Martin, Catherine, Albert, Pascale Martin and Catherine Camus, Albert's mother.

"I am touched that you have agreed to let me dedicate *Our Times* to you. I think I needed you with me this time." Letter from Albert Camus to René Char, 14 May 1950

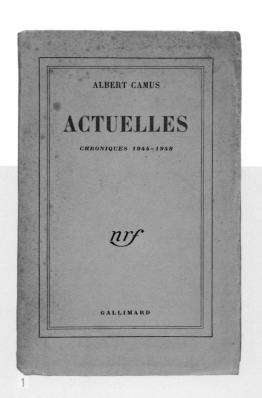

ALBERT CAMUS

ACTUELLES

CHRONIQUES 1944–1948

nrf

GALLIMARD

1

2

3

4

"To ask what is an absurd world
is to ask: 'Are we going to accept
hopelessness without doing anything
about it?' I don't think any honest
person can answer yes."
Notebooks 1935–1948, OCII, p. 1010

1- *Our Times I, Chronicles 1944–1948*, dedicated to René Char, was a collection of articles, mostly written for *Combat*, of which Camus was Editor from 1944 to 1947.

2- Camus in his office at home in the Rue Séguier in the 6th arrondissement of Paris in 1947.

3- Letter of thanks from René Char.

4- Autograph of the table of contents for *Our Times I, Chronicles 1944–1948*.

1- A profound study of rebellion, Camus's essay *Man as Rebel* provoked heated debate from the day it was published.

2- Camus in 1952.

3- Autograph of the contents pages of *Man as Rebel*.

"The first two cycles in my work deal with beings that know only honesty and are therefore not real people. They are not of the real world. That's probably why until now I haven't been a novelist in the conventional sense, but rather an artist who creates myths from his own passions and anxieties. It also explains why the people who have had the greatest impact on my life have always been those who had some kind of mythical power and focus."
Notebooks 1949–1959, OCIV, p. 1090

So, when revolutions succumb to the pressure of history and become murderous and arbitrary mechanisms, a new kind of rebellion is sanctified, in the name of reason and life.

We are at such a crisis point. Yet, inevitably, there is light even in the depths of the night and we can already see it; we have only to fight for it to appear.

Let us all look beyond this nihilism and, out of the ruins, prepare for a renaissance. But few are to know.
Man as Rebel, OCIII, p. 322

"Finished the first draft of *Man as Rebel*. This brings to an end the second cycle of my work. I'm 37. Will writing get easier now?"
Notebooks 1949–1959, OCIV, p. 1105

"I am doing nothing but work on *Man as Rebel*."
Letter from Albert Camus to René Char, February 1950

"The birth is proving to be long and difficult, and I think the baby will be ugly. The labour is exhausting."
Letter from Albert Camus to René Char, February 1951

1- Letter to Camus from René Char dated 16 July 1951.

2- Camus clenches his fist in rebellion.

3- Studio photograph of Camus in 1947.

Halfway through a century obsessed with making History and drowning in progressive delusions, Albert Camus shows us a way of thinking that makes History a subject for reflection: neither end nor means, History for Camus is no more than a path. He is convinced that rebellion is negated by crime, and nothing, not even for a moment, makes him deviate from this fundamental conviction.

Séverine Gaspari, *The Gift of Liberty: Albert Camus and the Libertarians*, published by Rencontres Méditerranéennes, 2008, p. 129

One of the answers Camus proposes to the tragic condition of man on earth is to accept that there are no absolutes. [...] Camus allows there to be uncertainty. [...] If it is to be true to its original purpose, a revolutionary act should be explainable in terms of relative values. It should remain faithful to the human condition. Though unswerving in its methods, it should accept that its ends can only be approximate and, in order for that approximation to become increasingly precise, should allow free discussion. In this way it would preserve the notion of a common man on whose behalf the revolution took place."

Séverine Gaspari, *The Gift of Liberty: Albert Camus and the Libertarians*, published by Rencontres Méditerranéennes, 2008, p. 133

"Thank you, my dear René, for your support. I have already expressed my gratitude for it and, to tell the truth, I needed it during this exhausting period of my life."

Letter from Albert Camus to René Char, 21 November 1951

"This proves that rebellion is the very motor of life and that whoever rejects it renounces life." *Man as Rebel*, OCIII, p. 322

"I am deeply immersed in your book and finding it moving, instructive and often shocking."
Letter from Louis Guilloux to Albert Camus, 21 December 1951

"Why am I a writer rather than a philosopher? Because I think in words, not in ideas."
Notebooks 1949–1959, OCIV, p. 1029

2

3

At the same time, the writer's role is necessarily a difficult task. By the nature of that role, he can no longer put himself at the service of those who would make History; he must serve those who suffer History. Otherwise, he would be isolated from his art and all the armies of all the tyrants in the world, with their millions of men, would not be able to save him from solitude, even though he had agreed to fall in step with them – or, rather, precisely because he had done so. But the silent suffering of an unknown prisoner, humiliated and ignored on the other side of the world, is enough to rescue the writer from exile, provided, of course, that he manages to ignore the privileges of freedom and pay attention to that silence so that his art can make it heard.

None of us is fitted for such a calling. But, whatever the circumstances of his life – whether he is unknown or temporarily famous, confined by the shackles of tyranny or free, for the time being, to express himself – the writer can find a sense of community with others that will justify his activity, on condition that he accepts, as far as he is able, the two duties that dignify his profession: to serve truth and to serve freedom. Since his calling is to unite as many people as possible, he can have no truck with deceit or servitude, which, wherever they hold sway, propagate isolation. Whatever our personal frailties, we will uphold the nobility of our profession by resolutely discharging two difficult responsibilities: refusing to lie about what we know to be true and resisting all oppression.

Swedish Speeches, OCIV, p. 240

Solitude and solidarity. 1952–1960

"Part of me has always utterly despised our era. Even in moments of direst need, I have never lost the taste for integrity, and my heart has often failed in the face of the extreme degeneration that has marked this century. But another part of me has always agreed to accept that degeneration and to take up the communal struggle against it [...]"
Notebooks 1949–1959, OCIV, p. 1129

1- Camus is confronted by the incomprehension of several of his contemporaries. André Breton, Jean-Paul Sartre and the publishers of the journal *Modern Times* cannot accept his condemnation of Marxism and its degeneration into totalitarianism. Camus opposes them, reasons with them, defends his position. In doing so, he is supported by several other artists and writers, including René Char and Louis Guilloux.

2, 3- In May 1952, *Man as Rebel* came to the attention of Francis Jeanson, a contributor to *Modern Times*. In his damning, almost insulting, critique he called it a "great failure". Camus addressed his response not to Jeanson but to Jean-Paul Sartre, the journal's Editor. There followed an exchange of letters in alternate issues. The rupture between the two men was definitive.

"What is your relationship now with your ex-colleague Jean-Paul Sartre?

– I have an excellent relationship with him, Sir, since the best relationships are those between people who never see each other. That said, the disagreement that caused the break between us has been greatly exaggerated in France, and perhaps also abroad. It was principally an ideological disagreement, in which we asserted positions that, naturally, in my opinion – and I'm sure you'll agree – are equally defensible. But diametrically opposed."

9 December 1957, *Swedish Speeches*, Appendices, OCIV, p. 286

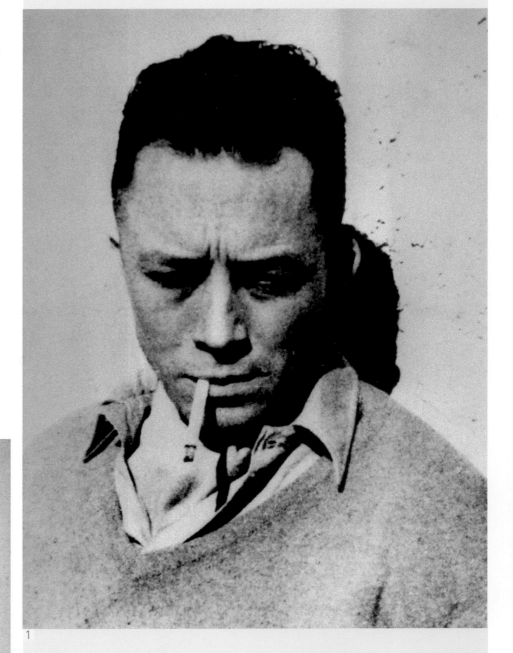

1

Les Temps Modernes

8ᵉ année   REVUE MENSUELLE   nᵒ 82

DIRECTEUR : *JEAN-PAUL SARTRE*

Août 1952

PAUL-ÉMILE VICTOR. — Natsek, la femme
qui n'avait ni cœur ni ventre.
LUIS MARTIN SERRANO. — Salazar sans masque.

DOCUMENTS

BLAKE. — Lettres d'un détenu américain.

EXPOSÉS

ÉTIEMBLE : Chronique littéraire. — De la prose française
au sabir atlantique.
ELENA DE LA SOUCHÈRE. — Les alternatives d'une négociation

CORRESPONDANCE

ALBERT CAMUS. — Lettre au directeur
des « Temps Modernes ».
JEAN-PAUL SARTRE. — Réponse à Albert Camus.
FRANCIS JEANSON. — Pour tout vous dire...

Rédaction, administration : 30, rue de l'Université, Paris

2

Pierre Bergé: Are you likely to write a sequel to *Man as Rebel*? Or might you wish to rework it in some way?

Albert Camus: I might write a sequel. But why should I rework it? I am not a philosopher and I have never claimed to be one. *Man as Rebel* does not pretend to be an exhaustive study of rebellion, which would therefore have to be added to and modified. I am aware of all the things it lacks in terms of facts and observations. But all I wanted to do was recount an experience, my own experience, which I know is shared by many others. In a certain way, the book is a confession – in fact, the only kind of confession I am capable of – and one that I took four years formulating, with all the polishing and refining that implies. I don't believe that my books should be taken in isolation. There are certain writers whose oeuvre seems to constitute a whole, in which each work is reflected in and illuminated by the others.

Our Times II – Letters on Rebellion, interview with Pierre Bergé, OCIII, p. 402

"I am waiting patiently for a catastrophe that is slow in coming."

December 1951, *Notebooks 1949–1959*, OCIV, p. 1119

3

Albert Camus.

CORRESPONDANCE

LETTRE AU DIRECTEUR
DES *TEMPS MODERNES*

Paris, le 30 juin 1952.

Monsieur le Directeur,

Je prendrai prétexte de l'article que, sous un titre ironique, votre revue m'a consacré, pour soumettre à vos lecteurs quelques observations touchant la méthode intellectuelle et l'attitude dont cet article témoigne. Cette attitude dont vous ne refusez pas, j'en suis sûr, d'être solidaire, m'intéresse plus en effet que l'article lui-même dont la faiblesse m'a surpris. Obligé de m'y référer constamment, je ne le ferai donc qu'après avoir précisé que je ne le considère pas comme une étude, mais plutôt comme un objet d'étude, je veux dire un symptôme. Je m'excuse enfin de devoir être aussi long que vous l'avez été. J'essaierai seulement d'être plus clair.

Mon premier effort sera de montrer quelle peut être l'intention réelle de votre collaborateur lorsqu'il pratique l'omission, travestit la thèse du livre qu'il se propose de critiquer et fabrique à son auteur une imaginaire biographie. Une question qui n'est secondaire qu'en apparence peut déjà nous mettre sur la voie d'une interprétation. Elle touche au bon accueil qui aurait été fait à mon livre par la presse de droite. La chose, en soi, ne m'aurait affligé que modérément. On ne décide pas de la vérité d'une pensée selon qu'elle est à droite ou à gauche et moins encore selon ce que la droite et la gauche décident d'en faire. A ce compte, Descartes serait stalinien et Péguy bénirait M. Pinay. Si, enfin, la vérité me paraissait à droite, j'y serais. C'est dire que je ne partage pas vos inquiétudes (ni celles d'*Esprit*) à ce sujet. Mais, de plus, ces inquiétudes me paraissent prématurées. Quelle a été en effet l'attitude de la presse dite de droite? Pour citer une feuille qui se tient résolument au-dessous des classifications politiques, j'ai été honoré d'une ration d'injures dans *Rivarol*. Du côté de la droite classique, *La Table Ronde*, sous la signature de M. Claude Mauriac, a eu de

Francis Jeanson.

POUR TOUT VOUS DIRE...

« La critique objective est pour moi la meilleure des choses et j'admets sans peine qu'on dise qu'une œuvre est mauvaise ou qu'une philosophie n'est pas bonne pour le destin de l'homme. Il est juste que les écrivains répondent de leurs écrits. Cela leur donne à réfléchir et nous avons tous un terrible besoin de réfléchir. »
Albert CAMUS, *Le pessimisme et le courage*.

« Quand on se laisse aller à présenter un spectacle ou à publier un livre, on se met dans le cas d'être critiqué et l'on accepte la censure de son temps. Quoi qu'on ait à dire, il faut alors se taire... »
Albert CAMUS, *Réponse à Gabriel Marcel* : « *Pourquoi l'Espagne?* ».

Bien que votre lettre, Albert Camus, ne parvienne à négliger mon article qu'au prix de s'en occuper vraiment beaucoup, le fait est que vous ne m'avez point écrit. Je vous répondrai donc. Cet article si faible, — au point que sa faiblesse est parvenue à vous surprendre, — il faut bien, quand vous l'attribuez à Sartre, que d'abord j'en revendique au moins le pire. D'autre part, je crois déceler entre nous une sorte de malentendu, et je suis d'autant plus soucieux d'y mettre fin que je m'en suppose en partie responsable : mes remarques, sans doute, auront manqué de netteté. Mais le mal n'est point sans remède, et je vais ici m'efforcer de ne plus vous décevoir.

Ces « embarras », précisément, où vous me voyez plongé, — une note au bas d'une page m'a ouvert les yeux sur le genre de méprise qui vous les a fait découvrir dans mon texte. Celui-ci, dites-vous, les « multiplie curieusement »; et vous y relevez un certain nombre d'expressions dont l'allure est en effet dubitative. Tout de même, Albert Camus, lorsque vous lisez : « il n'est pas sûr que... », ou : « comment se défendre de penser que... », ou encore : « je parviens mal, je l'avoue, à me dégager d'une telle interprétation, que tant de recoupements semblent confir-

Jean-Paul Sartre.

Mon cher Camus,

Notre amitié n'était pas facile mais je la regretterai. Si vous la rompez aujourd'hui, c'est sans doute qu'elle devait se rompre. Beaucoup de choses nous rapprochaient, peu nous séparaient. Mais ce peu était encore trop : l'amitié, elle aussi, tend à devenir totalitaire; il faut l'accord en tout ou la brouille et les sans-parti eux-mêmes se comportent en militants de partis imaginaires. Je n'y redirai pas : c'est dans l'ordre. Mais, précisément pour cela, j'eusse préféré que notre différend actuel portât sur le fond et que ne s'y mêlât pas je ne sais quel relent de vanité blessée. Qui l'eût dit, qui l'eût cru que tout s'achèverait entre nous par une querelle d'auteur où vous joueriez les Trissotin et moi les Vadius? Je ne voulais pas répondre : qui convaincrais-je? Vos ennemis à coup sûr, peut-être mes amis. Et vous, qui pensez-vous convaincre? Vos amis c'est mes ennemis. A nos ennemis communs, qui sont légion, nous prêterons l'un et l'autre à rire : voilà ce qui est certain. Malheureusement vous m'avez mis si délibérément en cause et sur un ton si déplaisant que je ne puis garder le silence sans perdre la face. Je répondrai donc : sans aucune colère mais, pour la première fois depuis que je vous connais, sans ménagements. Un mélange de suffisance sombre et de vulnérabilité a toujours découragé de vous dire des vérités entières. Le résultat c'est que vous êtes devenu la proie d'une morne démesure qui masque vos difficultés intérieures et que vous nommez, je crois, mesure méditerranéenne. Tôt ou tard, quelqu'un vous l'eût dit : autant que ce soit moi. Mais n'ayez crainte, je ne tenterai pas votre portrait, je ne veux pas encourir le reproche que vous faites gratuitement à Jeanson : je parlerai de votre lettre et d'elle seule, avec quelques références à vos ouvrages si c'est nécessaire.

Elle suffit amplement à montrer — s'il faut parler de vous comme l'anticommuniste parle de l'U.R.S.S.: hélas, comme *vous* en parlez — que vous avez fait votre Thermidor. Où est Meursault, Camus? Où est Sisyphe? Où sont aujourd'hui ces trotzkytes du cœur, qui prêchaient la Révolution permanente? Assassinés, sans doute, ou en exil. Une dictature violente et cérémonieuse s'est installée en vous, qui s'appuie sur une bureaucratie abstraite et prétend faire régner la loi morale. Vous avez écrit que mon collaborateur « voudrait qu'on se révoltât contre toute chose sauf contre le parti et l'État communistes » mais j'ai peur à mon tour

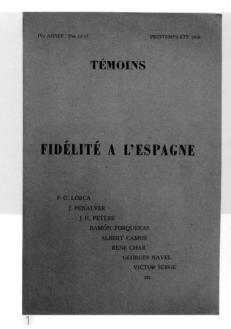

1

2

1- Issue 12 of the magazine *Witnesses*, entitled "Loyalty to Spain", to which Camus wrote the preface.

2, 3- In 1952, Franco's Spain was admitted to UNESCO. Camus resigned his UNESCO post and, on 30 November, delivered a diatribe on "Spain and her culture" at the Salle Wagram in Paris. The photograph shows him speaking, alongside Jean-Paul Sartre. Camus' ancestry linked him closely with Spain. As early as 1936, in the collective essay *Revolt in Asturias*, he denounced the Spanish government's response to the uprising of 30,000 Asturian miners.

4- The Order of the Spanish Liberation awarded to Camus on 2 January 1949.

5- Simone Weil joined the Durruti Column, an anti-Franco movement, during the Spanish Civil War. In 1946, as editor of Gallimard's *Collection Espoir*, Camus published eight of her works.

"I feel Spain's isolation deep inside me."
Notebooks 1949–1959, OCIV, p. 1129

3

4

Order of the Spanish Liberation. The Grand Chancellor of the Order certifies by the decree of 2 January 1949 that His Excellency the President of the Spanish Republic has expressed his wish that the Order of the Spanish Liberation be awarded to Mr Albert Camus, who shall thereby enjoy the privileges conferred upon its beneficiaries.

Today we celebrate another encouraging victory for democracy. But it is a victory over itself and at the expense of its own principles. Franco's Nationalists have sneaked into the cosy temple of culture and education while the Spain of Cervantes and Unamuno has once again been kicked into the street. Knowing that the current Minister of Information in Madrid, who is now UNESCO's direct contact, and the man who was in charge of Nazi propaganda under Hitler are one and the same, and that the government which has just honoured the Christian poet Paul Claudel is the very same government that awarded the Order of the Red Arrows to Himmler, who was responsible for the gas chambers, one may be justified in saying that it is not Calderon or Lope de Vega whom the world's democracies have just welcomed into their educational sanctum, but Joseph Goebbels. Seven years after the end of the war, we should congratulate M. Pinay's government for its splendid denial of the fact. Indeed, we should not reproach this honourable gentleman for having allowed such scruples to cloud his political judgement. We all thought, until now, that the progress of history depended at least in part on the tussle between teachers and executioners. It never occurred to us that this could be resolved simply by appointing executioners teachers. It occurred to M. Pinay's government.

Of course, the operation was a trifle embarrassing and had to be rushed through. But so what? After all, education is one thing and market forces are quite another! In this case, certainly, the forces are rather those of a slave market: the inhabitants of the colonies in exchange for the victims of the Fascist Phalanx. As for culture, that can wait. In any case, it is not the business of governments. Artists create culture and then governments control it, if necessary eliminating the artists in order to control it better, until the day arrives when a handful of military generals and industrialists start referring to "us" when talking of Molière and Voltaire or printing bowdlerized versions of the works of poets they have recently had shot. On that day, which has now arrived, we should spare a thought for poor old Hitler. Instead of committing suicide in an outburst of romanticism, all he had to do was hang around like his friend Franco. By now he would be UNESCO representative for Upper Niger, while Mussolini would be spending his time trying to instil some culture into the Ethiopian children whose fathers he decimated not so long ago. And so Europe would finally be reunited and the ultimate triumph of culture would be celebrated by a vast banquet at which generals and marshals would be served by a squad of democratic – but resolutely realist – ministers.

The word disgusting is inadequate to describe such a scene, but it seems pointless for us to keep reiterating our indignation. Since our governments are intelligent and realistic enough to think they can do without culture and integrity, let us ignore our feelings and ourselves be realistic. Since it is historical determinism that has brought Franco's Spain into UNESCO just eight years after the collapse of Europe's dictatorships amid the ruins of Berlin, let us remain objective and consider dispassionately the arguments of those who believe that Franco should remain in power.

Our Times II – Spain and Culture, speech given at the Salle Wagram on 30 November 1952, CCI I, p. 434

"Yes, the moment Franco's Spain became part of UNESCO, UNESCO ceased to be a part of world culture, and we should not be afraid to say so."

Our Times II – Spain and Culture, 30 November 1952, OCIII, p. 439

1- In 1951, Camus returned
   to his native country to
   "rediscover myself".

2- Camus dedicated *The
   First Man* to his mother,
   Catherine Sintès, "who
   will never be able to read
   this book [...]"

"My darling, sweet, innocent Mother, who was
stronger than time, stronger than history,
though it subjected you to it, and more genuine
than anything I have ever loved in this world, my
dear Mother, forgive your son for abandoning
you in your hour of darkness."

The First Man, Appendices, OCIV, p. 920

"When I am with my mother, I feel that I belong to a noble race: one that desires nothing."
Notebooks 1949–1959, OCIV, p. 1091

"And what he wanted more than anything in the world, which was for his mother to read everything he had written about his life and about his existence, was impossible. His love, his one and only love, would be forever unspoken."
The First Man, Appendices, OCIV, p. 930

"She raised her knotted hands to his face and caressed him."
The First Man, Appendices, OCIV, p. 927

L'ÉTÉ

PAR ALBERT CAMUS

LES ESSAIS LXVIII

nrf

GALLIMARD

"After fifteen years, I went back to my ruins, just a few yards from the sea's edge. I walked along the streets of the forgotten city, now covered with grass and spindly trees, and, on the slopes overlooking the bay, I once again ran my hands over the dough-coloured columns. But the ruins had been surrounded by barbed wire and access was restricted to a few gates."

Summer, Return to Tipasa, OCIII, p. 609

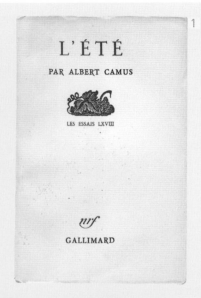

RETOUR A TIPASA

Tu as navigué, d'une âme furieuse loin de la demeure paternelle, franchissant les doubles rochers de la mer, et tu habites une terre étrangère.

MÉDÉE.

Depuis cinq jours que la pluie coulait sans trêve sur Alger, elle avait fini par mouiller la mer elle-même. Du haut d'un ciel qui semblait inépuisable, d'incessantes averses, visqueuses à force d'épaisseur, s'abattaient sur le golfe. Grise et molle comme une grande éponge, la mer se boursouflait dans la baie sans contours. Pourtant la surface des eaux était presque immobile sous la pluie fixe. De loin en loin seulement, un imperceptible et large mouvement soulevait au-dessus de la mer une vapeur trouble qui venait aborder sur le port, sous une ceinture de boulevards mouillés. La ville elle-même, tous ses murs blancs ruisselants d'humidité, exhalait une autre buée qui venait à la rencontre de la première. De quelque côté qu'on se tournât alors, il semblait qu'on respirât de l'eau, l'air enfin se buvait.

Devant la mer noyée, je marchais, j'attendais dans cet Alger de décembre, qui restait pour moi la ville des étés. J'avais fui la nuit d'Europe, l'hiver des visages. Mais la ville des étés elle-même s'était vidée de ses visages et ne m'offrait que des dos ronds et luisants. Le soir, dans les cafés violemment éclairés où je me réfugiais, je lisais mon âge sur des figures que je reconnaissais sans pouvoir les nommer. Je savais seulement que ceux-là avaient été jeunes avec moi, et qu'ils ne l'étaient plus.

Je m'obstinais pourtant, sans trop savoir ce que j'attendais, sinon que je voulais retourner à Tipasa. Certes, c'est une grande folie, et presque toujours châtiée, de revenir sur les lieux de sa jeunesse et de vouloir revivre à quarante ans ce qu'on a aimé dont on a fortement joui à vingt. Mais j'étais averti de cette folie. Une première fois déjà, j'étais revenu à Tipasa, peu après ces années de guerre qui marquèrent pour moi la fin de la jeunesse. J'espérais, je crois, y retrouver une liberté que je ne pouvais oublier. En ce lieu,

j'attendais, sinon, peut-être, le moment de retourner à Tipasa.

> "Amid the silence, amid the light, all the years of frenzy and darkness melted away and I heard within me a sound I had almost forgotten, as if, having stopped long ago, my heart were gradually beginning to beat again."

Summer, Return to Tipasa, OCIII, p. 612

-3-

Seine et leur parlaient à la fois de traditions et de conquête. Mais leur jeunesse les poussait à appeler cette compagnie. Il vient un temps, des époques, où elle est importune. "A nous deux", s'écrie Rastignac devant l'énorme moisissure de la ville parisienne. Deux, oui, mais c'est encore trop.

Le désert lui-même a pris un sens. On l'a surchargé de poésie; c'est un lieu consacré. Ce que le coeur demande à certains moments, ce sont justement des lieux sans poésie. Descartes ayant à méditer choisit son désert: la ville la plus commerçante de son époque. Il trouve sa solitude et l'occasion du plus grand, peut-être, de nos poèmes virils. C'est d'une main ferme qu'il trace alors sur le papier le meilleur de nos poèmes virils: "le premier (précepte) était de ne recevoir jamais aucune chose pour vraie que je ne la connusse évidemment être telle." On peut avoir moins d'ambition et la même nostalgie. Mais Amsterdam depuis trois siècles s'est couverte de musées. Pour fuir la poésie et retrouver la paix des pierres, il faut d'autres déserts, d'autres lieux sans âme et sans recours. Oran est l'un de ceux-là.

Il n'y a pas un lieu que les Oranais n'aient souillé par quelque hideuse construction qui devrait déshonorer n'importe quel paysage. On s'attend à une ville ouverte sur la mer, lavée, rafraîchie par des soirs. Et, mis à part le quartier espagnol, on trouve une cité qui présente le dos à la mer, qui s'est construite en tournant sur elle-même à la façon d'un escargot. Oran est un grand mur circulaire et jaune, recouvert d'un ciel dur. Au début, on erre dans le labyrinthe, on cherche la mer comme le signe d'Ariane. Mais on tourne en rond dans des rues fauves et oppressantes, et à la fin, le Minotaure dévore les Oranais: c'est l'ennui. Depuis longtemps, les Oranais ont accepté d'être mangés.

On ne peut pas savoir ce qu'est la pierre sans venir à Oran. Dans cette ville poussiéreuse entre toutes, le caillou est roi. On l'aime tant que les commerçants en mettent dans leurs

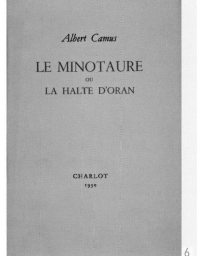

Albert Camus

LE MINOTAURE
OU
LA HALTE D'ORAN

CHARLOT
1950

1- In 1954, Gallimard published *Summer,* a collection of eight essays written by Camus between 1939 and 1953, most of which had previously been published separately: *The Minotaur or an Hour in Oran, The Almond Trees, Prometheus in Hell, Little Guide to Cities without a Past, Helen in Exile, The Enigma, Return to Tipasa* and *Close by the Sea.*

2, 5- The ruins at Tipasa, site of an ancient Roman town on the Algerian coast.

3- Page from the review *Terrasse* in which *Return to Tipasa* was first published in 1953 with corrections by Camus that were incorporated when it was republished as part of the collection *Summer.*

4- Typescript with handwritten corrections of *The Minotaur or an Hour in Oran.*

6- Camus visited Oran several times between 1939 and 1941. *The Minotaur or an Hour in Oran,* which was written in 1939, was first published by Charlot in 1950.

"Giving and receiving, aren't they the simple pleasures of life I referred to at the beginning? Yes, of course, they are life itself, vital and free, the life we all need."
Why I Write for the Theatre, OCIV, p. 610

1, 3- Camus taking part in rehearsals for the Angers Festival in 1953.

2- *Devotion to the Cross*, a play by Pierre Calderón de la Barca, written in 1633, was published by Camus in 1946 as part of the *Poetry and Drama* series he was editing for Éditions Charlot. It was then adapted for performance at the Angers Festival, with Maria Casarès and Serge Reggiani in the title roles.

4, 5- Front cover and programme for the 2nd Angers Festival in 1953, for which Camus adapted *Devotion to the Cross* by Pierre Calderón de la Barca and *The Spirits* by Pierre de Larivey, who, according to Camus, "was the most gifted of the dramatists who made the transition from the Italian to the classical style."

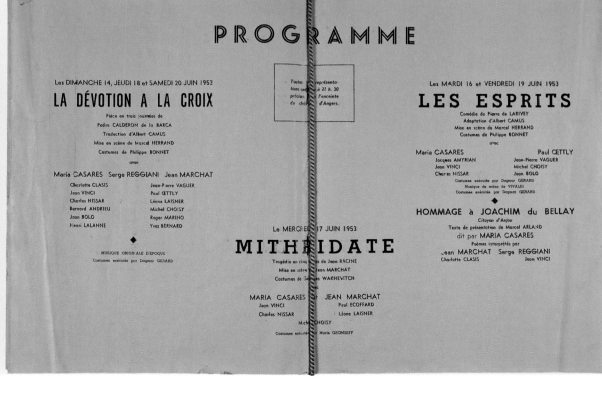

PROGRAMME

Les DIMANCHE 14, JEUDI 18 et SAMEDI 20 JUIN 1953

LA DÉVOTION A LA CROIX

Pièce en trois journées de
Pedro CALDERON de la BARCA
Traduction d'Albert CAMUS
Mise en scène de Marcel HERRAND
Costumes de Philippe BONNET

avec

Maria CASARES Serge REGGIANI Jean MARCHAT

Charlotte CLASIS   Jean-Pierre VAGUER
Jean VINCI   Paul ŒTTLY
Charles NISSAR   Léona LAISNER
Bernard ANDRIEU   Michel CHOISY
Jean BOLO   Roger MARINO
Henri LALANNE   Yves BERNARD

MUSIQUE ORIGINALE D'ÉPOQUE
Costumes exécutés par Dagmar GERARD

Le MERCREDI 17 JUIN 1953

MITHRIDATE

Tragédie en cinq actes de Jean RACINE
Mise en scène de Jean MARCHAT
Costumes de Georges WAKHEVITCH

avec

MARIA CASARES et **JEAN MARCHAT**

Jean VINCI   Paul ECOFFARD
Charles NISSAR   Léone LAISNER
Michel CHOISY

Costumes exécutés par Marie GROMSIEFF

Les MARDI 16 et VENDREDI 19 JUIN 1953

LES ESPRITS

Comédie de Pierre de LARIVEY
Adaptation d'Albert CAMUS
Mise en scène de Marcel HERRAND
Costumes de Philippe BONNET

avec

Maria CASARES   Paul ŒTTLY
Jacques AMYRIAN   Jean-Pierre VAGUER
Jean VINCI   Michel CHOISY
Charles NISSAR   Jean BOLO

Costumes exécutés par Dagmar GERARD
Musique de scène de VIVALDI
Costumes exécutés par Dagmar GERARD

HOMMAGE à JOACHIM du BELLAY

Citoyen d'Anjou
Texte de présentation de Marcel ARLAND
dit par MARIA CASARES
Poèmes interprétés par
Jean MARCHAT   Serge REGGIANI
Charlotte CLASIS   Jean VINCI

Toutes les représentations ont lieu à 21 h. 30 précises dans l'enceinte du château d'Angers.

1

"Yes, it's true, I generally denigrate the theatre, but that's because one tends to denigrate the things one is most passionate about. I've always been passionate about all aspects of the theatre – and not just as a writer, but as a director and an actor as well."

Swedish Speeches, 9 December 1957, Appendices, OCIV, p. 280

I chose the programme for the Angers Festival. I loved *The Knight of Olmedo* and I wanted to give people a chance to get to know the great Spanish plays, which are little known in France, either because they haven't been translated or because they've been translated badly. As far as my own career is concerned, I decided when I was adapting *Requiem* for the stage that I would start directing again. And I'll continue to do so as long as I'm asked. But I'd really like to have my own theatre company. I have specific ideas as to what the theatre should be about and how actors should act. I'd like to put my ideas into practice."
Interview for *Paris-Théâtre*, OCIV, p. 580

1, 2- Camus at a rehearsal for *Devotion to the Cross*.

3- Poster for the 2nd Angers Festival, which ran from 14 to 20 June 1953.

1- On 17 June 1953, rioting
    broke out in East Berlin
    as workers protested
    against the communist
    regime. Here, demon-
    strators throw stones at
    Soviet tanks outside the
    Ministry of the Economy
    in Wilhelmstraße.

2- Camus spoke out against
    communist repression in
    East Berlin.

To make my position clear, I must say first of all that certain people took a rather disgusting satisfaction in what happened in Berlin – a satisfaction that we cannot possibly share. At the same time as the Rosenbergs, after two years of suffering, were being taken to the electric chair, the news that the Russian army was firing at workers in East Berlin, far from making us forget the Rosenbergs' agony, as the so-called bourgeois press tried to do, merely added to our sense of the relentless misery of a world in which, one by one, all our hopes are being systematically exterminated.

Freedom Diary, 17 June 1953, OCIII, p. 925

2

"When a worker, anywhere in the world, raises his bare fists against a tank and shouts that he is not a slave, what sort of people are we if we do nothing about it? [...] Yet it is precisely such indifference that we have just witnessed, and that is why it is not merely indignation but disgust that prompts us to speak to you tonight."

Speech at the Maison de la Mutualité, 17 June 1953, OCII, p. 926

"I defy those who say publicly that they don't know enough about these events to admit the same to themselves when they are alone in the face of death."

Freedom Diary, 17 June 1953, OCIII, p. 927

You all know about
the 12th World War.

LA DOUZIÈME GUERRE MONDIALE,
COMME CHACUN SAIT,

Which destroyed
the whole human
civilisation
and all culture.

AMENA L'ÉCROULEMENT DE LA CIVILISATION.

One day a girl saw the
last surviving flower.
She had seen a flower
for the first time.

UN JOUR, UNE JEUNE FILLE QUI N'AVAIT
JAMAIS VU DE FLEUR VINT A TOMBER SUR
LA DERNIÈRE QUI POUSSAIT EN CE MONDE.

The boy and the girl
tended the last flower.
Soon the flower
blossomed.

LE JEUNE HOMME ET LA JEUNE FILLE
SOIGNÈRENT ENSEMBLE LA FLEUR
QUI COMMENÇA DE REVIVRE.

Very soon those who
went to the plains
started feeling they
should have gone to
the hills.

MAIS ALORS, CEUX QUI VIVAIENT DANS LES
VALLÉES REGRETTÈRENT DE N'AVOIR PAS
CHOISI LES COLLINES.

1- Pages from Camus's
translation of James
Thurber's *The Last
Flower*, with its legendary
illustrations, which Gal-
limard published in 1952.

2- Camus in 1952.

1

"The morning after a great historical crisis, you feel as sad and sick as after a heavy night. But there is no aspirin for historical hangovers."

Notebooks 1949–1959, OCIV, p. 1179

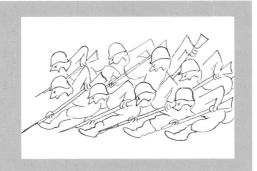

ET, A L'INSTANT, LE MONDE FUT DE NOUVEAU EN GUERRE.

Once again the world plunged into war.

I left Tipasa once again and returned to Europe and its conflicts. But the memory of that day still gives me support and helps me to confront with equanimity those things that bring joy and those that bring grief. In these difficult times, what more could I want than to learn to ignore nothing and to spin both black and white into a single thread and stretch it until it almost breaks? It now seems to me that both forces, however contradictory, have been at work in everything I have done and said until now. I have neither rejected the light into which I was born nor ignored the oppressions of my time. It would be facile to contrast the tranquillity of Tipasa with the names of places that resound with brutality. Suffice it to say that we must follow a path through our world, a path that I know only too well, which leads to the hills of the human spirit but also to the valleys of criminality. And we have a choice: we can relax and snooze on the hills or we can lodge in the valleys. But if we ignore one or the other, we cease to be; we cease to live and to love, except by proxy. It is therefore this will to live without denying anything that exists that I value more than anything in this world. There are times, I admit, when I would have liked to exercise that will. Precisely because few eras have required men to face up to such extremes of good and evil as ours, I would like nothing to escape me and to retain a dual memory. On the one hand there is beauty and on the other there are the downtrodden. However difficult the undertaking, I would like to remain faithful to both.

Summer, Return to Tipasa, OCIII, p. 613

INTRODUCING Disney's *THE LIVING DESERT*

Water is all around us. Billions of human beings are squeezed onto strips of land surrounded by oceans, which cover two-thirds of the globe. What we call continents are in fact islands assaulted by storms and hurricanes, eaten away by rain discharged by saturated clouds onto the countries of which we briefly claim ownership. Thus we spread and multiply on lands that are gradually being eroded and impoverished. Soon there will be too many people for the world to support and freedom will exist only on the seas and in the deserts. For the time being, though, our hardships make us stronger; we stand fast to face the enemy. Wherever water falls, trees grow, so that a thick carpet covers the earth and men gather and prosper. But where there is no water, men die or flee and the parched earth is left to the wind. This is how deserts are born, arid oases, kingdoms where harsh freedom reigns, inhospitable places in which men may yet manage to find a refuge from their overpopulated islands.

These silent, desiccated countries are dotted about the globe and from time to time small groups of men cross them without ever settling. But where no man can live, some perhaps can learn about life. Indeed, the murderous terrain and the frightening solitude of the world's great deserts – the Sahara, the Kalahari, the Gobi, the great American desert and those of Arabia, Persia and Australia – can teach those who wish to learn that the human spirit languishes in comfort and thrives amid privation. In these strange lands, life derives a sudden nobility from danger and destitution. If, as Heraclitus believed, the *soul* is improved by desiccation, then the soul that is consumed by desert dryness is god of the world.

The Living Desert, OCIII, p. 938

1

1 to 3- In 1954, Disney produced a book containing stills from the film *The Living Desert*. The eponymous book contained texts by Julian Huxley, Marcel Aymé, Louis Bromfield, François Mauriac, André Maurois and Henri de Montherlant, as well as Camus, whose two contributions were entitled *Introducing the Desert* and *Rain and Flowering*.

"Who could tolerate discrimination and hatred, let alone survive in the desert that is in us all, without the imperious obstinacy that refuses to give in and treats death itself as a triumph? Our deserts are therefore the kingdoms of that unique virtue, which exists of itself and without which no other virtue can exist, the will to live."

The Living Desert, OCIII, pp. 941–943

In these sterile plains, nothing will ever grow that could be useful to man; not a single grain would ripen into corn among its stony furrows. Every living thing is born fully formed, struggles briefly from its first to its last breath and then dies, without knowing youth or old age and without resignation. Nothing here is latent; everything simply is, all at once. But even though there is no hope, yet there is beauty, fleetingly miraculous and eternally dazzling. Deserts are places of beauty, pointless but irreplaceable. Their only crops are flowers that have but a day or two in which to germinate, bloom and vanish. Yet their sudden sprays of multicoloured poppies and campanulas are resplendent even as they fade and die. Some plants wait a full ten years before flowering. Then they blossom and disappear in a single day.

The Living Desert, OCIII, p. 942

s'épanouissent et meurent en un jour. Comment certains hommes n'adoreraient-ils pas dans ces fleurs une énigme fraternelle? Non, il n'est pas de créature si ingrate qu'une rosée fugace un jour ne la fasse fleurir et ne l'emplisse d'un lait de douceur. Le cactus du désert se couvre d'épines, s'engonce dans sa carapace pustuleuse, et le voilà semblable à une affreuse plante animale, arbre sans ombre, pieuvre prisonnière, enchaînée par malédiction dans l'enfer du soleil et de la poussière. Vienne la pluie pourtant, et sous son brusque baptême, la peau maintenant verte et vernissée du cactus se soulève, crève, et laisse s'échapper une à une les plus belles fleurs du désert. Au premier soleil, elles dardent timidement le fourreau encore froissé de leurs pétales couverts de rosée. Le soleil les sèche rapidement et à mesure que la journée avance, la corolle s'ouvre un peu, se défroisse, se déploie encore. Sur ces plantes mortes éclate enfin une fête somptueuse de couleurs et de chairs tendres : des corolles fragiles veinées d'un sang léger dorment dans un lit d'épines. Et comme certains visages hirsutes et ravinés offrent la surprise d'un regard clair et tendre, ici des végétaux maudits

60

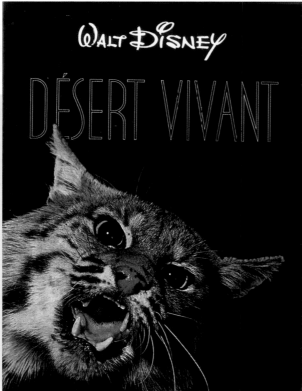

3

2

"But life in the desert teaches us to accept with equal gratitude destitution and profusion. [...] Who in such solitude, whether created by nature or by society, could live and create without divine resolution?"
The Living Desert, OCIII, pp. 941–943

"I have always had the feeling of being on the high seas: elated but in mortal danger."

Notebooks 1949–1959, OCIV, p. 1107

1- Camus at the home of Michel and Janine Gallimard in Sorel-Moussel, in the department of Eure-et-Loir, in the summer of 1957.

2- Francine and Albert at Le Panelier.

3 to 5- Catherine, Jean and Albert on holiday in Sorel-Moussel.

"'The modern city alone,' Hegel opined, 'offers the human spirit the environment in which he can come to terms with himself.' It would seem that we are living in the era of the metropolis. Our world has wittingly cut itself off from the very things that ensure its permanence: nature, the sea, the mountains, the quiet of the evening."
Summer, Helen in Exile, OCIII, p. 599

3

4

5

1, 2- Camus at Les Brefs,
        the property belonging
        to Michel Gallimard's
        mother, in 1947.

3, 4- Jean and Catherine
        Camus in Sorel-Moussel.

5- Catherine Camus at
     Lourmarin in Provence.

The end.

Give back the land, as the land belongs to no one. Give back the land, which can be neither bought nor sold (and the reason Christ never came to Algeria is that the monks owned it and decided who should be admitted).

And looking first at his mother, then at the others, he cried: 'Give back the land. Give it all to the poor, to those who have nothing and are so poor that they have never even wanted to own or to possess, to those who are like her, the impoverished masses of this country, most of them Arabs but some French, who live or survive here through stubbornness and stamina, the poor, whose dignity is the only dignity worthy of the name. Give them the land, as what is sacred is given to the sacred, so that I shall be poor again, cast into the humblest exile in the furthest corner of the earth, and may smile and die happy, knowing that the land I so loved and the people I so revered have been reunited under my native sun.

(Anonymity will have borne fruit and will engulf me. I will again be part of this country.) [...]

The First Man, Appendices, OCIV, p. 944

"Newspapers do not tell the truth by supporting revolution. They support revolution by telling the truth."

Notebooks 1949–1959, OCIV, p. 1131

"There was nothing either in the subject of Albert Camus's article or in the dispassionate manner in which he discussed it that could in any way justify such an avalanche of outrage."
La Gazette de Lausanne, 28–29 January 1956

L'Express **Trêve pour les civils** MARDI 10 JANVIER 1956

par ALBERT CAMUS

Il n'y a pas de jour où le courrier, la presse, le téléphone même, n'apporte de terribles nouvelles d'Algérie. De toutes parts, les appels retentissent, et les cris. Dans la même matinée, voici la lettre d'un instituteur arabe dont le village a vu quelques-uns de ses hommes fusillés sans jugement, et l'appel d'un ami pour ces ouvriers français, tués et mutilés sur les lieux mêmes de leur travail. Et il faut vivre avec cela, dans ce Paris de neige et de boue, où chaque jour se fait plus pesant !

Si, du moins, une certaine surenchère pouvait prendre fin ! À quoi sert désormais de brandir les uns contre les autres les victimes du drame algérien ? Elles sont de la même tragique famille et ses membres aujourd'hui s'égorgent en pleine nuit, sans se reconnaître, à tâtons, dans une mêlée d'aveugles.

Cette tragédie d'ailleurs ne fait pas pleurer tout le monde. On en voit qui exultent, quoique de loin. Ils sermonnent, mais sous leurs airs graves, c'est toujours le même cri : « Allons ! encore plus fort ! Voyez comme celui-ci est cruel, crevez-lui donc les yeux ! » Hélas, s'il est encore en Algérie des hommes qui aient du retard dans cette course à la mort et à la vengeance, ils le rattraperont à toute allure. Bientôt l'Algérie ne sera peuplée que de meurtriers et de victimes. Bientôt les morts seuls y seront innocents.

★

Je sais : il y a une priorité de la violence. La longue violence colonialiste explique celle de la rébellion. Mais cette justification ne peut s'appliquer qu'à la rébellion armée. Comment condamner les excès de la répression si l'on ignore ou l'on tait les débordements de la rébellion ? Et inversement, comment s'indigner des massacres des prisonniers français si l'on accepte que des Arabes soient fusillés sans jugement ? Chacun s'autorise du crime de l'autre pour aller plus avant. Mais à cette logique, il n'est pas d'autre terme qu'une interminable destruction.

« Il faut choisir son camp », crient les repus de la haine. Ah ! je l'ai choisi ! J'ai choisi mon pays, j'ai choisi l'Algérie de la justice, où Français et Arabes s'associeront librement ! Et je souhaite que les militants arabes, pour préserver la justice de leur cause, choisissent aussi de condamner les massacres des civils, comme les Français, pour sauver leurs droits et leur avenir, doivent condamner ouvertement les massacres répressifs.

★

Du moins, il faut faire vite. Chaque jour qui passe ruine un peu plus l'Algérie et voue ses masses à des années de misère supplémentaires. Chaque mort sépare un peu plus les deux populations ; demain, elles ne s'affronteront plus d' part et d'autre d'un fossé, mais au-dessus d'une fosse commune. Quel que soit le gouvernement qui, dans quelques semaines, abordera le problème algérien, il risque alors de se trouver devant une situation sans issue.

Il revient donc aux Français d'Algérie eux-mêmes de prendre les initiatives nécessaires. Ils craignent Paris, je le sais, et ils n'ont pas toujours tort. Mais que font-ils pendant ce temps, que proposent-ils ? S'ils ne font rien, d'autres feront pour eux, et pourquoi se plaindraient-ils ensuite ? On me dit que certains d'entre eux, éclairés d'une brusque lumière, ont choisi de soutenir Poujade. Je ne veux pas encore croire à ce qui serait un suicide pur et simple. L'Algérie a besoin d'esprit d'invention, non de slogans périmés. Elle meurt, empoisonnée par la haine et l'injustice. Elle se sauvera seulement en neutralisant sa haine par une surabondance d'énergie créatrice.

★

C'est pourquoi il faut s'adresser une fois de plus aux Français d'Algérie pour leur dire : « Tout en défendant vos maisons et vos familles, ayez la force supplémentaire de reconnaître ce qui est juste dans la cause de vos adversaires, et de condamner ce qui ne l'est pas dans la répression. Soyez les premiers à proposer ce qui peut sauver l'Algérie et établir une loyale collaboration entre les fils différents d'une même terre ! » Aux militants arabes, il faut tenir le même langage. Au sein même de la lutte qu'ils soutiennent pour leur cause, qu'ils désavouent enfin le meurtre des innocents et qu'ils proposent, eux aussi, leur plan d'avenir !

À tous, il faut enfin crier trêve. Trêve jusqu'au moment des solutions, trêve au massacre des civils, de part et d'autre ! Tant que l'accusateur ne donne pas l'exemple, toutes les accusations sont vaines. Amis français et arabes, ne laissez pas sans réponse un des derniers appels pour une Algérie vraiment libre et pacifique, bientôt riche et créatrice ! Il n'y a pas d'autre solution, il n'y a aucune autre solution que celle dont nous parlons. Au-delà d'elle, il n'y a que mort et destruction. Des mouvements se constituent partout, je le sais, des hommes de courage, arabes et français, se regroupent. Rejoignez-les, aidez-les de toutes vos forces ! Ils sont le seul, et le dernier espoir, de l'Algérie.

A. C.

(Copyright L'Express.)

Albert Camus en Alger pour une trève civile

Dialogue pour la Paix en Algérie

COMMUNAUTÉ
algérienne

DOCUMENTATION · CONFRONTATION · SYNTHÈSE

JUSTICE SOCIALE · DÉMOCRATIE POLITIQUE

► A son appel, 800 Algériens de toutes les origines, rassemblés malgré d'odieuses provocations, déclarent :

L'exposé d'Albert Camus

Un bel exemple de résolution et de calme

L'intervention du Pasteur Capieu

L'exposé d'Albert Camus

UN APPEL DE SIMPLE HUMANITÉ...

Un bel exemple de résolution et de calme

Pendant qu'il conviait à la paix...

(SUITE A LA PAGE 2).

"You will find it easy to believe me if I say that I suffer for Algeria as others suffer from bronchitis. [...] My whole life (and you know how much it hurt me to leave my country), I have supported the idea that far-reaching reforms were needed, but others denied it and continued to pursue the dream of power, which thinks it is eternal. [...] That is why I am solidly behind you in what you want to do, my dear Kessous."

Letter from Albert Camus to Mohamed Aziz Kessous, 20 September 1955

1- On 22 January 1956, Camus intervened in the Algerian war of independence to call for an end to violence against civilians. He expressed his views in a number of articles published in *L'Express*.

2, 3- At the same time, Camus supported Mohamed Aziz Kessous in his attempt to launch a newspaper entitled *Communauté algérienne*.

4- Camus in Paris in the 1950s.

> "But when Camus came into the print room, it was as if it had suddenly been illuminated by a ray of sunshine."

To Albert Camus from his Friends at the Press, 1962

> "The problem is not that intellectuals are avoiding journalism. It is that they are rushing into it and writing anything and everything just to earn money or, still less excusable, to get their name in print."

One of the Finest Professions I Know…, OCIII, p.880

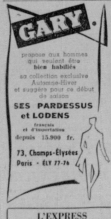

nrf

24 novembre 1957

Merci de tout cœur, mon cher Roy, et à toi et à votre camarade, de ton mot d'amitié. Les honneurs valent ce qu'ils valent, et aussi ce que valent les hommes que les donnent. Mais ce fut une de mes fiertés que d'avoir gardé l'estime et la sympathie d'hommes comme toi qui ont longtemps travaillé au même métier que moi. Je vous serre la main à vous les deux, avec amitié

Albert Camus

1- Camus in the print room of *L'Express* with the typesetter Georges Roy, with whom he had worked at *Combat*. Behind them is the paper's publisher Philippe Grimbach.

2- Letter to Georges Roy.

3- On 25 October 1955, Camus explains the position he had adopted in his writing on the Franco-Algerian conflict.

> "Don't wait for the Last Judgement; it happens every day."
>
> *The Fall*, OCIII, p. 748

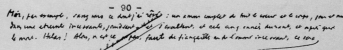

> "Where is the dividing line between confession and accusation? Is the narrator of this story putting himself on trial or the time in which he is living? One thing is clear in any case, in this clever game of mirrors: suffering, and what it brings."
>
> *The Fall*, Notes, OCIII, p. 771

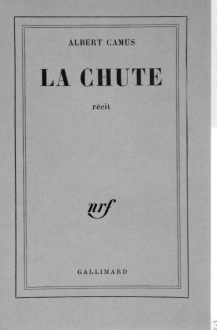

1- The Mexico-City bar in Amsterdam, where the protagonist of *The Fall*, former Parisian lawyer Jean-Baptiste Clamence, begins to recount his life story.

2- Typescript of *The Fall* with handwritten corrections.

3- In 1956, Camus published *The Fall*, an enigmatic tale that takes the form of a long monologue in which the protagonist searches for a lost innocence, a paradise he wishes to rediscover. According to the then Director of the Swedish Academy, Ake Erlandsson, it was the publication of *The Fall* that persuaded the jury to award the Nobel Prize to Camus.

4- Camus on the balcony at the offices of Gallimard.

"It was at that moment that my daily life was suddenly invaded by thoughts of death. [...] And I became tormented by the idea that I would not have time to finish the task I had set myself."

The Fall, OCIII, p. 737

"Look, it is snowing! Oh, I must go outside!
Amsterdam asleep under a white blanket, the
canals glowing in the dark like jade beneath
their little snowy bridges, the streets deserted,
my footsteps muffled: it will be a moment of
purity before tomorrow's slush. Look at the
huge snowflakes splattering on the windows.
They must be the doves of peace."
The Fall, OCIII, p. 764

1- Camus in Montroc near Chamonix in 1956.
2- Aerial view of Amsterdam.
3- Covers of foreign editions of *The Fall*.

"Have you noticed that Amsterdam's canals are concentric, like the circles of hell? Bourgeois hell, of course, haunted by bad dreams."

The Fall, OCIII, p. 702

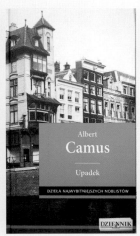
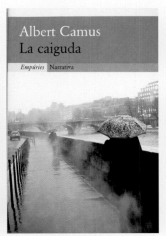
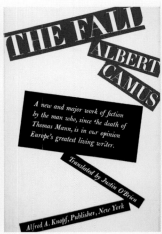

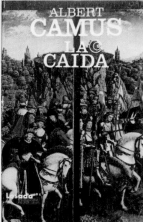

> "*Requiem* is therefore, in my opinion, one of the few modern tragedies."
>
> *Requiem for a Nun*, Appendices, OCIII, p. 844

There are seven principal characters. First, a young couple: the man elegant and unconventional, who will be portrayed by Michel Auclair, the woman slightly frivolous and to be played by Catherine Sellers. As for the 'nun', she will be personified by Tatiana Moukhine. Marc Cassot will be the young couple's uncle, the lawyer and 'driver' of the action, and Michel Maurette will play the governor of the State of Virginia. François Dalou, as the young gangster, and Jacques Gripel, as the prison warden, a sinisterly comic figure, will provide the light-hearted interludes in this crime drama, which reaches its climax on the eve of an execution.

Requiem for a Nun, Appendices, OCIII, p. 848

1- Camus with Catherine Sellers and Marc Cassot in a rehearsal of Camus's stage adaptation of Faulkner's *Requiem for a Nun*. The play, which was first performed in 1956, was success.

2- Camus outside the Théâtre des Mathurins.

3- Camus with Catherine Sellers.

4- Camus during a workshop.

> "I am a great admirer of William Faulkner, whose work I have known and studied for a long time. In my opinion, he is your greatest writer [...]"
>
> *Requiem for a Nun*, Appendices, OCIII, p. 841

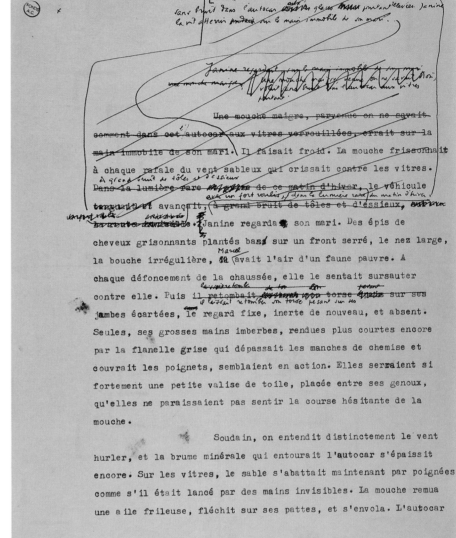

1- In 1957, Gallimard published *Exile and the Kingdom*, a collection of six texts written between 1952 and 1956: *The Adulterous Woman*, *The Renegade or a Lost Soul*, *The Silent Ones*, *The Guest*, *Jonas or the Artist at Work* and *The Stone that Grew*. It was dedicated to Francine.

2- Annotated typescript of the first page of *The Adulterous Woman*.

3, 4- Autograph title page of *Exile and the Kingdom* and first proof with annotations.

5- *The Adulterous Woman*, with illustrations by Pierre-Eugène Clairin, published by Noël Schumann in 1954.

6- Autograph title page of *The Adulterous Woman*.

7, 8- Revisions to the first paragraph of *The Adulterous Woman*.

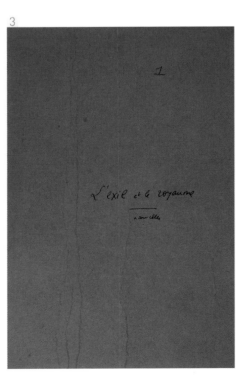

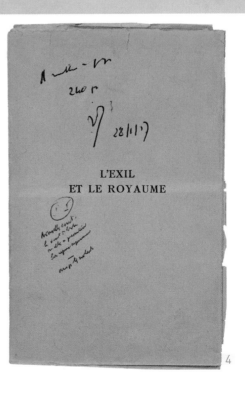

"Since the beginning of time, a few men have wandered ceaselessly across the parched, bone-dry earth of this endless country, owning nothing and serving no one, masters of a strange kingdom, poor but free."

Exile and the Kingdom, The Adulterous Woman, OCIV, p. 13

"And then, as I read on, an unexpected feeling came over me, a feeling I hadn't had in a long time and which silenced criticism."

Letter from Jean Grenier to Albert Camus, 25 April 1955

nrf

99 - 100

Accroupi au bord du plateau, l'instituteur contemplait l'étendue déserte. Il hésitait et il fallait pourtant se décider. Daru avait trop vécu avec les enfants pour supporter qu'on les tue, ce meurtre devant cette chétée. On ne peut pas tout pardonner, tout confondre, toujours, la victime et l'assassin, on ne peut pas vivre sans une loi, commune à tous et sur laquelle on puisse se battre alors jusqu'à la mort. On ne pouvait pas vivre sans honneur..... De l'autre côté de l'école le prisonnier tournait. Daru l'écouta, presque malgré lui, puis, furieux, jeta un caillon qui siffla dans l'air avant de s'enfoncer dans la neige. Il se leva. Se battre était une chose, livrer un homme, fut-il aussi criminel que celui-ci en était une autre qui n'avait rien à voir avec l'honneur. D'y penser seulement le rendait fou d'humiliation. Et il maudissait à la fois les siens qui lui envoyaient cet homme et celui-ci dont le crime imbécile le révoltait. Mais à ce moment, Daru sentit l'expression d'effroi de violence qu'avait eue l'Arabe à son réveil. Il ne pouvait chasser cette image, elle lui était insupportable. Il tourna en rond sur le terre-plain, attendit, immobile, puis entra dans l'école.

Paris, 17, rue de l'Université — 5, rue Sébastien-Bottin (VIIᵉ)

- I4 -

que la semaine prochaine tout irait mieux. "Tu m'inviteras." dit-il. Saïd sourit. Il ~~mangeait maintenant~~, mais légèrement, comme un homme sans faim.

Esposito prit une vieille casserole et alluma un petit feu de copeaux et de bois. Il fit réchauffer du café qu'il avait apporté dans une bouteille. Il dit que c'était un cadeau pour l'atelier que lui avait fait son épicier quand il avait appris de la grève. Un verre à moutarde circula de main en main. A chaque fois, Esposito versait le café déjà sucré. Saïd l'avala avec plus de plaisir qu'il n'avait mis à manger. Esposito buvait le reste du café à même la casserole brûlante, avec des clappements de lèvres et des jurons. A ce moment, Ballester entra pour annoncer la reprise.

Pendant qu'ils se levaient et rassemblaient papiers et vaisselles dans leurs musettes, Ballester vint se placer au milieu d'eux et dit soudain que c'était un coup dur pour tous, et pour lui aussi, mais que ce n'était pas une raison pour se conduire comme des enfants et que ça ne servait à rien de bouder. Esposito, la casserole à la main, se tourna vers lui; son épais et long visage avait rougi d'un coup. Yvars savait ce qu'il allait dire, et que tous pensaient en même temps que lui, qu'ils ne boudaient pas, qu'on leur avait fermé la bouche, c'était à prendre ou à laisser, et que l'impuissance font parfois si mal qu'on ne peut même pas crier. Ils étaient des hommes, voilà tout, et ils n'allaient pas se mettre à faire des sourires et des mines. Mais Esposito ne dit rien de

"When he woke up, he could hear no movement in the classroom. He was surprised to feel a rush of joy at the thought that the Arab had managed to escape and that he would be left alone without having to make any decisions. But his prisoner was still there. He had simply stretched out between the stove and the desk."

Exile and the Kingdom, The Guest, OCIV, p. 52

"[...] Rateau looked at the canvas, which was entirely blank apart from a single word in the centre, which Jonas had written so small that it was difficult to tell whether it read 'solitary' or 'solidarity'." *Exile and the Kingdom, Jonas or the Artist at Work*, OCIV, p. 83

1- Autograph of *The Guest*.
2- Annotated typescript of *The Guest*.
3- *The Guest* – scene from the comic book by Jaques Ferrandez (2009)
4- Handwritten revision to *The Renegade or the Lost Soul*.
5- Autograph title page of *The Renegade or the Lost Soul*.
6- Annotated proofs of the title page of *Jonas or the Artist at Work*.
7- Camus in 1957.

"He was just starting to eat when he noticed Saïd on a pile of wood shavings a few feet away, lying on his back and staring up at the glass roof, through which he could see that the sky was now a duller blue. He asked him if he had already eaten. Saïd replied that he had had some figs. Yvars stopped eating. The uneasy feeling he had had since the interview with Lassalle suddenly disappeared, giving way to a pleasant warmth. He got up, broke his sandwich in half and, when Saïd declined the offer, said that next week things would be a lot better. 'It'll be your turn to make the offer,' he said. Saïd smiled and took part of Yvars' sandwich, which he nibbled at, like a man who had lost his hunger."
Exile and the Kingdom, The Silent Ones, OCIV, pp. 41–42

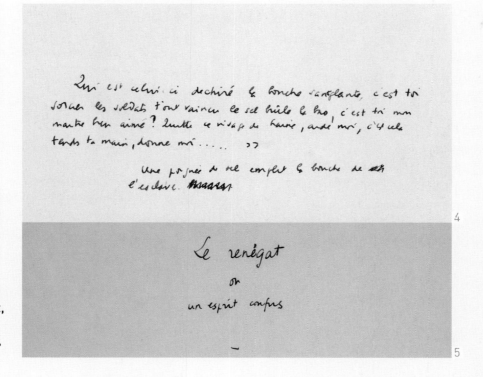

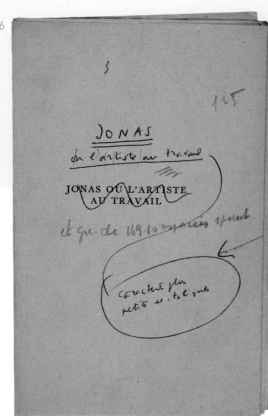

"'It's nothing,' said the doctor they had called a few moments later. 'He's been working too hard. He'll be back on his feet next week.'

'Are you sure he'll get better?' said Louise, her face haggard."
Exile and the Kingdom, Jonas or the Artist at Work, OCIV, p. 82

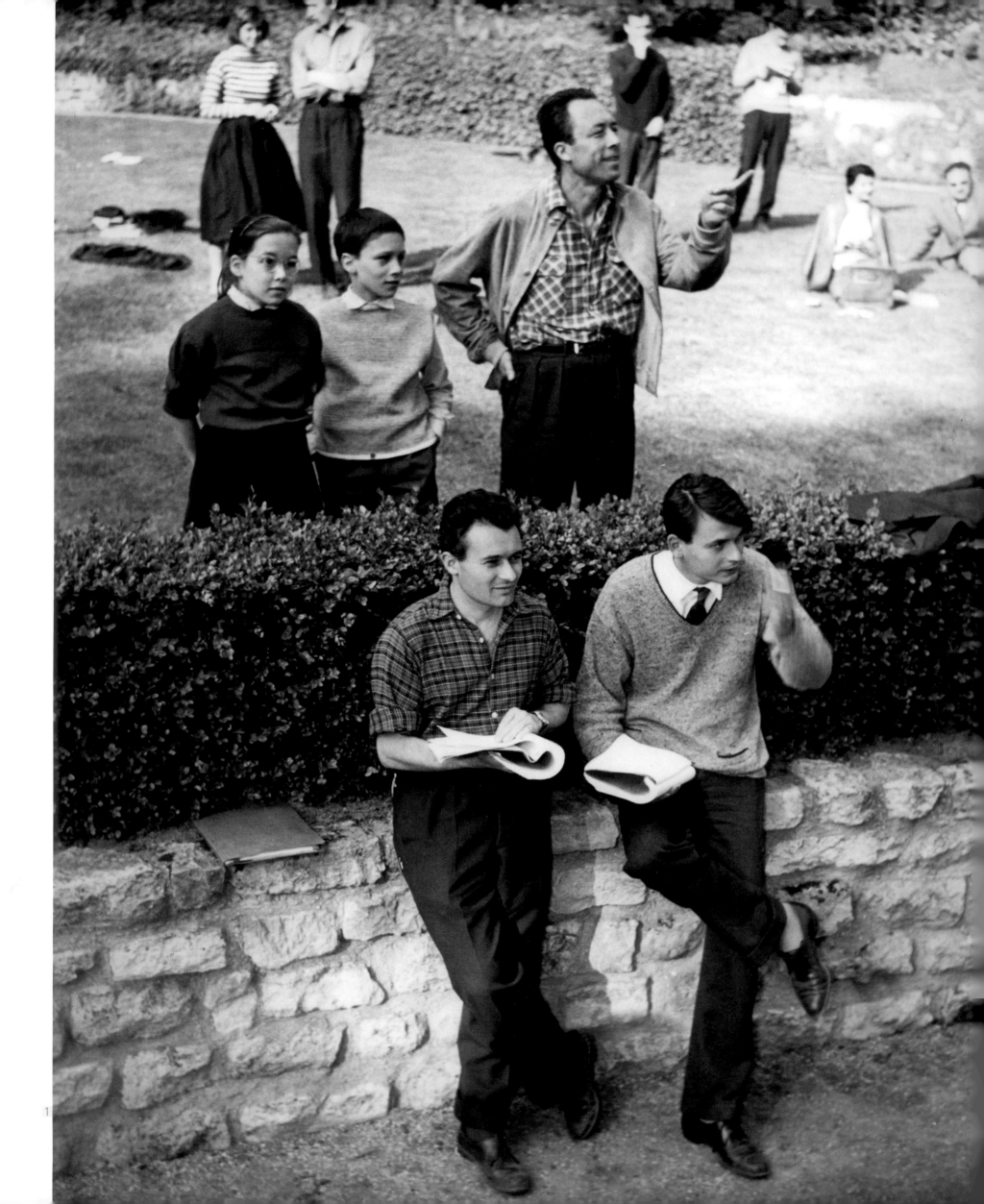

2　　　　　3　　　　　4

1 to 5- Camus with his children Catherine and Jean at a rehearsal of *The Knight of Olmedo* at the Pré Catelan restaurant in Paris.

6- Camus with Jean-Pierre Marielle, Dominique Blanchar, Catherine Camus and Catherine Sellers.

Heroism, tenderness, beauty, honour, mystery and fantasy – everything that ennobles human destiny and makes life passionate – run throughout the play and constantly remind us of the importance of this period in Spanish theatre, which today tends to be hidden away in cupboards and attics. Now that Europe has been reduced to ashes, Lope de Vega and his fellow dramatists can bring us their inextinguishable brilliance, their unique vitality, and help us to rediscover a sense of grandeur that will enable our theatre to develop and progress.

The Knight of Olmedo, Introduction, OCIV p. 172

"At the very least, I hope that audiences will be impressed by the vitality and intensity of this play, which is one of Lope de Vega's most successful and often brings to mind *Romeo and Juliet* in its intertwining of themes of love and death."

The Knight of Olmedo, Introduction, OCIV p. 172

"He was not a seducer, he was a seductive man, which is not the same thing at all [...] His charm was his simplicity."

Catherine Sellers, *Interview with Joël Calmettes*, 2009

5

6

1- Poster for the 6th Angers Festival, in 1957, at which he presented a revised version of *Caligula* and a new production of *The Knight of Olmedo*.

2- Rehearsing on a rainy day at the Bagatelle Hotel. Camus is in the centre.

3- Camus directs a rehearsal of *The Knight of Olmedo* for the 1957 Angers Festival.

"Often, when I write a play, it is the writer in me who is at work, following a carefully constructed overall plan. When I adapt a play, it is the director who is working, in accordance with his ideas about the theatre. In fact, I believe in creating a total spectacle, conceived, inspired and shaped by the same mind, written and directed by the same person, which generates unity of tone, style and rhythm – the crucial ingredients of a show."
Why I Write for the Theatre, OCIV, p. 609

ANGERS
1957

VIᵉ FESTIVAL D'ART DRAMATIQUE

1

"Angers Festival over. Tired and happy. Life, wonderful life, with its injustices, its glories, its passions, its struggles, life starts again and I must find the strength to love everything and to create all-encompassingly."
Notebooks 1954–1958, OCIV, p. 1257

"I received the news with a kind of panic. What is helping me through it are the gestures of people I love." Letter from Albert Camus to Nicola Chiaromonte, 20 October 1957

1 to 4- On 17 October 1957, the Permanent Secretary of the Swedish Academy, Anders Oesterling, announced on the radio that the Nobel Prize in Literature had been awarded to Albert Camus "for his extensive body of literary work, which illuminates the principal questions facing man today". Camus was 44. Here he and Francine are attending the award ceremony at the offices of Gallimard, where Camus is interviewed by a journalist.

"In any case, I must overcome this strange terror, this incomprehensible panic, which this unexpected announcement has thrown me into."
Notebooks 1949–1959, OCIV, p. 1267

French Press Agency communiqué
Albert Camus awarded Nobel Prize in Literature

Stockholm, 17th October (AFP)

At 3 p.m. today the Swedish Academy gathered in the Nobel Library of the Stockholm stock exchange to award the 1957 Nobel Prize in Literature, whose recipient, as the Academy's Secretary General, Anders Oesterling, announced to the assembled Swedish and foreign journalists at 3.14 p.m. precisely, was Albert Camus.

In accordance with the regulations, Oesterling stated, the decision had been made by consensus of the members of the Academy.

1-   Camus, winner of the
      Nobel Prize in Litera-
      ture, and his wife Fran-
      cine, are congratulated
      by the Swedish Ambas-
      sador to France, Ragnar
      Kumlin, at the Gallimard
      reception on 17 October
      1957.

2, 3- Camus at the offices
       of Gallimard after the
       announcement of his
       Nobel Prize win.

"Terrified by what is happening to me, which I didn't ask for. What makes it worse is the vilification, which is like a kick in the stomach."
Notebooks 1949–1959, OCIV, p. 1266

"I decided I would accept not only the invitation to Stockholm but also all the duties that go with it. [...] It seems to me that one should play the game according to the rules. [...] Your friendly letter warmed my heart."
Letter from Albert Camus to Roger Martin du Gard (winner of the 1937 Nobel Prize in Literature), 20 November 1957

"But for the last few years Camus seems to have been resting on his laurels; his recent works (*The Fall* and *Exile and the Kingdom*) are unlikely to attract new readers to him. One wonders whether Camus is already over the hill and whether the Swedish Academy, thinking it was honouring a young writer, has not in fact set the seal on his premature ossification."
Roger Stéphane, *L'Observateur*, 24 October 1957

"It should come as no surprise that an institution which values the ideas behind a writer's work more than its quality [...] should be irresistibly attracted to a man who hobbles along the literary road using capital letters as crutches: Human Conscience, Dignity (likewise Human), Liberty, Hope. [...] It should be remembered that the Academy has the unfailing knack of identifying when a writer's work – be it Hemingway's, Gide's, Mauriac's – is finished, or practically finished. Those who are surprised that Camus has been honoured by the Academy at such a young age are forgetting this sixth sense and the fact that its decision indicates that they consider Camus to be finished. It will be no great loss."
Jacques Laurent, *Arts*, 23 October 1957

"I think I am rather young. Personally, I would have voted for Malraux. Nevertheless, I am grateful to the Nobel jury for having chosen to honour an Algerian-French writer. I have never written anything that was not, in one way or another, connected with the land in which I was born. It is therefore to that land, and to its sufferings, that my thoughts are directed."

Swedish Speeches, Appendices, OCIV, p. 272

"Nobel Prize. Overwhelmed by a strange feeling of melancholy. When I was 20, poor and unencumbered, I knew what true glory was. My mother." *Notebooks 1949–1959*, OCIV, p. 1266

1- Camus and Francine in the train on their way to Stockholm in December 1957.

2- Camus with Janine Gallimard in the restaurant car of the train.

3- On the ferry from Denmark to Sweden.

4- Camus passing the bust of Alfred Nobel on his way to the press conference held on the eve of the award ceremony.

5- Camus with the Mayor of Stockholm.

3

5

4

"Three suffocating attacks of panic and
claustrophobia in one month. Off balance. [...]
More worried than ever."
Notebooks 1949–1959, OCIV, p. 1267

Camus at the press conference held on 9 December 1957, the day after his arrival in Stockholm.

– Mr Camus, which of the characters you have created do you feel speaks the most plainly and directly, with the voice of Albert Camus?

– You know, it's a difficult question to answer, because I've always felt that all the characters a writer creates represent one or other of his temptations. For me, a writer is a creator of life. I say writer because I am a writer. I should say: "An artist is a creator of life." And the writer himself is, of course, a life. By 'life' I mean a multi-faceted force that can follow several...that can follow several paths, that is tempted by everything around him. That's why I can't say which of my characters could be considered my spokespeople. I feel as if I am all of them, even those who might seem less likeable than others.

Swedish Speeches, Press conference in Stockholm, 9 December 1957, OCIV, p. 280

At the same time, having emphasized the nobility of the writer's vocation, I should have put him in his proper place, alongside his fellow fighters, and with no greater claim to honorifics than them, carrying on his work without shame, nor pride in being in the public eye, constantly treading the line between suffering and beauty, and dedicated above all to drawing from his double personality creations that he stubbornly strives to protect from the ravages of history. Who, then, could possibly expect him to provide ready-made answers and satisfying morals? The truth is mysterious and elusive, impossible to pin down. Freedom is dangerous and as arduous as it is elating. We must advance towards these two goals, haltingly but resolutely, knowing in advance that we will falter somewhere along the road.

Swedish Speeches, OCIV, p. 242

"Above all, I feel solidarity with the common man."

Interview for the newspaper *Demain*, October 1957

1- Francine at the Nobel Prize award ceremony.

2- Facsimile of Nobel Prize in Swedish, awarded to Camus on 10 December 1957.

3- Camus steps up to give his acceptance speech on 10 December 1957.

4, 5- The King of Sweden, Gustav VI, and dignitaries applaud at the end of Camus's speech.

6- Francine with the King of Sweden, Gustav VI.

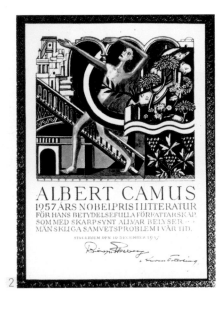

"The great artist walks along a high ridge; each step is both adventurous and extremely dangerous. Yet it is his willingness to expose himself to that danger that constitutes his freedom as an artist."

Swedish Speeches, *The Artist and His Time*, Speech delivered at Uppsala University on 14 December 1957, OCIV, p. 262

The secret of every great work of art is that it enriches and ennobles the human condition. And all the concentration camps and prison bars in the world are not enough to obliterate these overwhelming testimonies to dignity. That is why it is not possible, as some would have us believe, to repress a culture, even temporarily, in order to create a new one. Man's incessant testimony to his own suffering and grandeur cannot be repressed. There is no culture without a past and we neither can nor should reject any aspect of our own culture, that of the Western world. Whatever form the art of the future may take, it will necessarily be the product of the same elements; it will be made of the courage and freedom that have been nourished by the bravery of thousands of artists of every century and every nationality. Yes, when today's tyrants tell us that artists, even if they confine themselves to their art, are public enemies, they are right. But in doing so they also pay homage to an image of man that nothing has ever been able to eradicate.

Swedish Speeches, *The Artist and His Time*, Speech delivered at Uppsala University on 14 December 1957, OCIV, p. 263

1-Albert and Francine prepare to face the photographers.

2-Camus at a reception at Stockholm's town hall.

3-Camus with (from left to right) Janine Gallimard, Francine Camus, and Claude, Simone and Michel Gallimard.

4-Albert and Francine with Claude and Michel Gallimard (right).

"Novelists, playwrights and philosophers have always been committed without reservation to bringing out what is best in man and to opposing everything that tries to crush, sully or deride it. In doing so, they have instinctively defended their ideas and their means of expression from the vulgarizing and banalizing effects of progress, standardization, politics and polemics, not to mention propaganda."
Swedish Speeches, Appendices, OCIV, p. 273

"I am tired of living, acting, feeling in a certain way in order to prove other people wrong. I am tired of living according to the image others have of me. I have decided to be autonomous, to claim my independence, even in the midst of our interdependence."

The First Man, Appendices, OCIV, p. 923

1- Camus signing books labelled "Nobel Prize".

2- In June 1958, Camus spent a month travelling around Greece with Maria Casarès and Michel and Janine Gallimard.

Myths have no life of their own. They wait for us to embody them. It needs only one person in the world to answer their call and their sap rises at once. We must therefore preserve that sap and make sure that, when it falls, it does not die so that it may rise again. I sometimes wonder whether we have the right to save humanity today. But it is surely possible to save its children, both their bodies and their spirits. It is surely possible to give them the chance of being happy and of appreciating beauty.

Summer, Prometheus in Hell, OCIII, p. 591

"We have banished beauty. The Greeks took up arms to defend it."   *Summer, Helen in Exile,* OCIII, p. 597

"Delphi. Once again the extraordinary terraced ascent towards the light. I seem to be treading in my own footsteps."
Notebooks 1949–1959, OCIV, p. 1281

"In the theatre, we are forced to work together because … as I will explain in a moment, there is nevertheless a feeling a solidarity among us, but as I was saying, we are forced to work together because the fruit of two months of labour on a project such as this is something we enjoy either collectively or not at all."

The Possessed, Appendices, OCIV, p. 540

> "*The Possessed*, by Dostoyevsky, is in my opinion one of the four or five greatest works ever written." *The Possessed*, Appendices, OCIV, p. 537

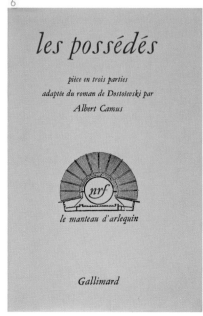

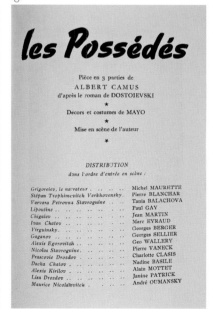

1- In 1959, Camus directed his own adaptation of Fyodor Dostoyevsky's *The Possessed*. The scenery and costumes were designed by Mayo, and the premiere took place on 30 January at the Théâtre Antoine in Paris. Here Camus is seen at a rehearsal.

2- Roger Blin and Pierre Vaneck in *The Possessed*.

3- Jeanine Patrick, Catherine Sellers, Pierre Vaneck and Nadine Basile.

4- Camus with Pierre Blanchar and Jeanine Patrick.

5- Camus working with Tania Balachova.

6- Cover of *The Possessed* ("a play in three acts adapted from the novel by Dostoyevsky by Albert Camus"), published by Gallimard in 1959 under its imprint *Le Manteau d'Arlequin*.

7- A portrait of Dostoyevsky – along with that of another Russian master, Tolstoy – hangs permanently in Camus's office "because he teaches us what we know but refuse to admit".

8- The cast list, which included Tania Balachova, Catherine Sellers, Pierre Blanchar, Pierre Vaneck and Alain Mottet.

1, 2- Camus at the Théâtre
Antoine, where *The Possessed* was playing, on
20 April 1959.

"The book *must be* unfinished."

The First Man, OCIV, p. 927

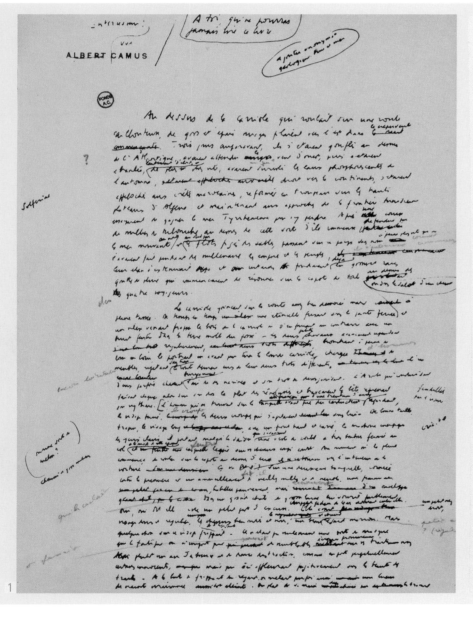

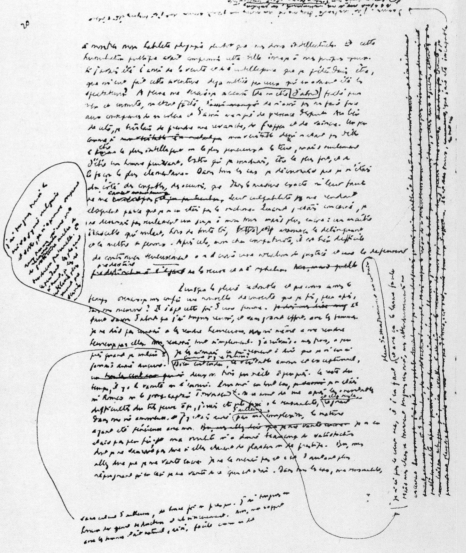

"Started work again. Have made progress with first part of *First Man*. Thanks to this landscape, its solitude, its beauty."

Notebooks 1949–1959, OCIV, p. 1296

"Lourmarin. First evening here after so many years. The first star over the Luberon, the vast silence, the top of the cypress tree rocking me to sleep, the countryside solemn and austere despite its overwhelming beauty."

Notebooks 1935–1948, OCII, p. 1067

"Even my death will be controversial. Yet my most profound desire is for a quiet death, which will leave those whom I love in peace." *Notebooks 1949–1959*, OCIV, p. 1299

1- On 4 January 1960, Camus, Michel and Janine Camus and their daughter travelled up from Lourmarin to Paris by car. Near Villeneuve-la-Guyard, in the department of Yonne, Michel Gallimard's Facel Vega went off the road and hit a tree. The two men were killed. Janine and her daughter escaped death.

2- Camus was buried in Lourmarin cemetery.

ETERNITY IN LOURMARIN

When someone leaves us, there is no longer a straight road to follow, no longer any lights to show us the way. Where can we bury our love? He continues to circle us, constantly eluding our grasp. His face occasionally brushes against ours, leaving only an icy scar. Never again will there be a day when our happiness can be prolonged; every aspect of his presence – and there were almost too many to count – has been torn from us at a stroke. Vigilance becomes routine ... And yet this extinguished being remains within us, clinging to something solid, naked, essential, the eternity we have spent together reduced to the thickness of an eyelid.

We have stopped talking to the person we loved but there is still a sound to be heard. What is it? We know, or think we know. But only when the familiar opens the door to the past to let him through. Now he is beside us, now further away, now just in front.

It is in this newly intimate moment, when the full weight of the mystery oppresses us with questions, that pain suddenly strikes, the pain of separation, which the arrow of time can no longer pierce.

René Char, *Eternity in Lourmarin*, OC IV, p. 412

And he himself [...] like a naked and vibrant blade destined to be snapped irreparably in two, his pure passion for life extinguished by sudden death, could already feel his life, his youth, his loved ones slipping away from him, without any hope of saving them, and abandoned himself to the blind hope that this obscure force, which for so many years had carried him far above the everyday and nourished him boundlessly so that he was equal to the harshest circumstances, would continue to provide for him, and with the same unstinting generosity as it had shown in giving him reasons to live, reasons to grow old and reasons to die without protest.

The First Man, OCIV, p. 914

Albert Camus and
Michel Gallimard.

"Although it was the middle of winter, I finally realized that, within me, summer was inextinguishable." *Summer, Return to Tipasa*, OCIII, p. 613

Bibliography

The complete works of Albert Camus are published by Gallimard, in the series La Pléiade and Folio.

References to Camus's works in this volume correspond to:

ALBERT CAMUS, *Œuvres complètes I, 1931–1944, II, 1944–1948*, edited by Jacqueline Lévi-Valensi (2006), Paris: Gallimard, Bibliothèque de la Pléiade.

ALBERT CAMUS, *Œuvres complètes III, 1949–1956, IV, 1957–1959*, edited by Raymond Gay-Crosier (2008), Paris: Gallimard, Bibliothèque de la Pléiade.

The translation of *L'Étranger* (*The Outsider*) quoted here was previously published by Penguin Books and is reproduced by kind permission of the publishers. All other translations were made specifically for this edition.

CAMUS'S PUBLISHED WORKS (IN CHRONOLOGICAL ORDER):

(The English translations of the titles of Camus's works used in this volume are the present translator's and may not correspond to the titles of published translations; they are given in brackets below following the original French titles.)

Collective work (1936) *Révolte dans les Asturies* (*Revolt in Asturias*). Algiers: Edmond Charlot.

ALBERT CAMUS (1937) *L'Envers et l'Endroit* (*Back and Front*). Algiers, Méditerranéennes.

ALBERT CAMUS (1937) *Noces* (*Nuptials*). Algiers: Edmond Charlot.

ALBERT CAMUS (1942) *L'Étranger* (*The Outsider*). Paris: Gallimard.

ALBERT CAMUS (1943) *Le Mythe de Sisyphe* (*The Sisyphus Myth*). Paris: Gallimard.

ALBERT CAMUS (1944) *Le Malentendu* and *Caligula* (*The Misunderstanding* and *Caligula*). Paris: Gallimard.

ALBERT CAMUS (1945) *Lettres à un ami allemand* (*Letters to a German Friend*). Paris: Gallimard.

ALBERT CAMUS (1947) *La Peste* (*The Plague*). Paris: Gallimard.

ALBERT CAMUS (1948) *L'État de Siège* (*State of Siege*). Paris: Gallimard.

ALBERT CAMUS (1950) *Les Justes* (*The Just*). Paris: Gallimard.

ALBERT CAMUS (1950) *Actuelles I – chroniques, 1944–1948* (*Our Times I – Chronicles 1944–1948*). Paris: Gallimard.

ALBERT CAMUS (1951) *L'Homme révolté* (*Man as Rebel*). Paris: Gallimard.

ALBERT CAMUS (1952) *La Dernière Fleur*, translation of *The Last Flower*, an illustrated fable by James Thurber. Paris: Gallimard.

ALBERT CAMUS (1950) *Actuelles II – chroniques, 1948–1953* (*Our Times II – Chronicles 1948–1953*). Paris: Gallimard.

ALBERT CAMUS (1953) *Les Esprits* (*The Spirits*), play in three acts adapted from Pierre de Larivey. Paris: Gallimard.

ALBERT CAMUS (1953) *La Dévotion à la croix* (*Devotion to the Cross*), play in three parts translated and adapted from the play *La Devoción de la Cruz* by Pedro Calderón de la Barca. Paris: Gallimard.

ALBERT CAMUS (1954) *L'Été* (*Summer*). Paris: Gallimard.

The Living Desert (1954): Foreword by Walt Disney, text by Marcel Aymé, Louis Bromfield, Albert Camus, Julian Huxley, François Mauriac, André Maurois and Henry de Montherlant. Paris: Société française du livre.

ALBERT CAMUS (1955) *Un Cas intéressant* (*An Interesting Case*), play in two parts and eleven scenes adapted from the play *Un Caso Clinico* by Dino Buzzati. Paris: L'Avant Scène.

ALBERT CAMUS (1956) *La Chute* (*The Fall*). Paris: Gallimard.

ALBERT CAMUS (1956) *Requiem pour une nonne* (*Requiem for a Nun*), play in two parts and seven scenes adapted from the novel by William Faulkner. Paris: Gallimard, Le Manteau d'Arlequin.

ALBERT CAMUS (1957) *L'Exil et le Royaume* (*Exile and the Kingdom*). Paris: Gallimard.

ALBERT CAMUS and ARTHUR KOESTLER (1957) *Réflexions sur la peine capitale* (*Reflections on Capital Punishment*), with an introduction and commentary by Jean Bloch-Michel. Paris: Calmann-Lévy, Liberté de l'esprit.

ALBERT CAMUS (1957) *Le Chevalier d'Olmedo* (*The Knight of Olmedo*), drama in three parts translated and adaptated from the play *El Caballero de Olmedo* by Lope de la Vega. Paris: Gallimard.

ALBERT CAMUS (1958) *Discours de Suède* (*Swedish Speeches*). Paris: Gallimard.

ALBERT CAMUS (1958) *Actuelles III – chroniques algériennes, 1939–1983* (*Our Times III – Algerian Chronicles 1939–1958*). Paris: Gallimard.

ALBERT CAMUS (1959) *Les Possédés* (*The Possessed*), play in three parts adapted from the novel by Fyodor Dostoyevsky. Paris: Gallimard, le Manteau d'Arlequin.

Posthumous Publications

ALBERT CAMUS (1962) *Carnets I, mai 1935–février 1942* (*Notebooks I, May 1935–February 1942*). Paris: Gallimard.

ALBERT CAMUS (1962) *Théâtre, récits, nouvelles* (*Plays, Essays & Novels*), edited by Roger Quillot. Paris: Gallimard, Bibliothèque de la Péiade.

ALBERT CAMUS (1964) *Carnets I, janvier 1942–mars 1951* (*Notebooks II, January 1942–March 1951*). Paris: Gallimard.

ALBERT CAMUS (1965) *Essais* (*Essays*), edited and annotated by Roger Quilliot and Louis Faucon and with an introduction by Roger Quilliot. Paris: Gallimard, Bibliothèque de la Pléiade.

ALBERT CAMUS (1971) *La Mort heureuse* (*A Happy Death*), with an introduction and notes by Jean Sarocchi. Paris: Gallimard, Cahiers Albert Camus I.

PAUL VIALLANEIX (ed.) (1973) *Le Premier Camus* (*Early Camus*) and *Écrits de jeunesse* (*Youthful Works*). Paris: Gallimard, Cahiers Albert Camus 2.

ALBERT CAMUS (1978) *Journaux de voyage* (*Travel Diaries*), edited and annotated by Roger Quilliot. Paris: Gallimard.

JACUELINE LÉVI-VALENSI and ANDRÉ ABOU (eds) (1978) *Fragments d'un combat, 1938–1940, Alger républicain, Le Soir républicain* (Fragments of a Combat, *Alger républicain* and *Le Soir républicain*). Paris: Gallimard, Cahiers Albert Camus 3 (1–2).

ALBERT CAMUS and JEAN GRENIER (1981) *Correspondance, 1932–1960* (*Correspondence 1932–1960*), with an introduction and notes by Marguerite Dobrenn. Paris: Gallimard.

ALBERT CAMUS (1986) *La Postérité du soleil* (*After the Sun*) with photographs by Henriette Grindat and *Itinéraires* (*Travels*) by René Char. Vevey: Éditions de l'Aire.

PAUL-F. SMETS (ed.) (1987) *Albert Camus éditorialiste à l'Express, mai 1955–février 1956* (*Albert Camus as Contributor to l'Express, May 1955–February 1956*). Paris: Gallimard, Cahiers Albert Camus 6.

ALBERT CAMUS (1989) *Carnets III, mars 1951–décembre 1959* (*Notebooks III, March 1951–December 1959*). Paris: Gallimard.

ALBERT CAMUS (1994) *Le Premier Homme* (*The First Man*). Paris: Gallimard.

ALBERT CAMUS (196) *Carnets* (*Notebooks*). Paris: Gallimard, Cahiers Albert Camus 7.

ALBERT CAMUS and PASCAL PIA (2000) *Correspondance, 1939–1947* (*Correspondence 1939–1947*), edited by Yves Archenbaum. Paris: Fayard/Gallimard.

JACQUELINE LÉVI-VALENSI (ed.) (2002) *Camus à Combat, éditoriaux et articles d'Albert Camus 1944–1959* (*Camus at Combat, editorial and articles 1944–1959*). Paris: Gallimard, Cahiers Albert Camus 8.

ALBERT CAMUS and RENÉ CHAR (2007) *Correspondance, 1949–1959* (*Correspondence 1949–1959*), with an introduction and notes by Franck Planeille. Paris: Gallimard.

CAMUS IN ENGLISH

The following is a selection of published translations of works by Camus and books about Camus and his work in English.

ALBERT CAMUS, *Caligula and other plays*, trans. Stuart Gilbert. London: Penguin.

ALBERT CAMUS, *Exile and the Kingdom*, trans. Carol Cosman. London: Penguin.

ALBERT CAMUS, *The Fall*, trans. Justin O'Brien. London: Penguin.

ALBERT CAMUS, *The First Man*, trans. David Hapgood. London: Penguin.

ALBERT CAMUS, *A Happy Death*, trans. Richard Howard. London: Penguin.

ALBERT CAMUS, *Lyrical and Critical Essays*, trans. Ellen Conroy Kennedy. London: Vintage.

ALBERT CAMUS, *The Myth of Sisyphus*, trans. Justin O'Brien. London: Penguin.

ALBERT CAMUS, *Notebooks 1935–1942*, trans. Philip Thody. Lanham, MD: Ivan R. Dee.

ALBERT CAMUS, *Notebooks 1942–1951*, trans. Justin O'Brien. Lanham, MD: Ivan R. Dee.

ALBERT CAMUS, *Notebooks 1951–1959*, trans. Ryan Bloom. Lanham, MD: Ivan R. Dee.

ALBERT CAMUS, *The Outsider*, trans. Joseph Laredo. London: Penguin.

ALBERT CAMUS, *The Plague*, trans. Robin Buss. London: Penguin.

ALBERT CAMUS, *The Rebel*, trans. Anthony Bower. London: Penguin.

DAVID CARROLL (2008) *Albert Camus the Algerian, Colonialism, Terrorism, Justice*. Columbia University Press.

CHRISTINE MARGERRISON, MARK ORME and LISSA LINCOLN (eds) (2008) *Albert Camus in the 21st Century: A Reassessment of His Thinking at the Dawn of the New Millennium*. Amsterdam: Rodopi.

JOHN FOLEY (2008) *Albert Camus, From the Absurd to Revolt*. Stockfield: Acumen Publishing.

PHILIP THODY (1973) *Albert Camus 1913–60*. London: Hamish Hamilton.

OLIVIER TODD (1997) *Albert Camus, A Life*. Knopf/Vintage.

ROBERT ZARETSKY (2010) *Albert Camus, Elements of a Life*. Cornell University Press.

Acknowledgements

The publication of this homage to Albert Camus would not have been possible
without the assistance of:

Catherine Camus, his daughter, who confided in us, revealed her souvenirs to us
and dedicated her heart and mind to the production of this book.

Elisabeth Masondieu-Camus, his granddaughter, for her support throughout the
project.

Le Centre de Documentation Albert Camus in Aix-en-Provence, whose archivist
Marcelle Mahasela allowed us to plunder its treasures.

Éditions Gallimard and its president Antoine Gallimard, who gave us permission to
reproduce texts by their illustrious author.

To all of them we extend our heartfelt thanks.

Picture Credits

Michel Lafon would like to thank Bernard Mahasela for his invaluable assistance in reproducing documents from the collection of Catherine and Jean Camus.

Position on page:
b = bottom, t = top
l = left, c = centre, r = right,

© 1704/Gamma/Eyedea Presse: p. 75t.

© AFP/D.R.: pp. 182l, 183, 200l.

© Albert Harlingue/Roger Viollet: pp. 90r, 91b, 91tr.

© ALTITUDE/Arthus-Bertrand Yann: p. 169t.

© Archives Gallimard/Koestler: pp. 126, 127r.

© Archives Nationales d'Outre-mer: pp. 15tl, 36tl, 54bl, 55r, 57.

© Bénisti: pp. 33b, 37, 38r, 53b.

© Bernand/CDDS Bernand: pp. 115r, 148, 149t, 150, 151t, 170, 176, 177.

© Bernard Mahasela/Aix-en-Provence: pp. 28tl, 34br, 42b, 48b, 51b, 65c, 67, 77c, 78br, 79cl, 80l, 87b, 98tl, 98b, 99b, 101br, 127ct, 132r, 136, 146tl, 149b, 162b, 163, 165r, 198l, 199bl, 199br.

© Bernard Rouget/Rouget family/website: www.bernardrouget.com: pp. 51r, 86, 92bl, 93.

© Bettmann/Corbis: pp. 5cr, 44, 109g, 179.

© Bibliothèque Nationale de France: p. 20b.

© Brassaï/Réunion des Musées Nationaux: pp. 80–81.

© Bridgeman/Giraudon/Albrecht, Wolfgang, Deutsches Historisches Museum, Berlin: p. 152.

© Catherine and Jean Camus, private collection. Albert Camus Foundation. Méjanes Library, Aix-en-Provence. Rights reserved: pp. 10, 11l, 11c, 12t, 13, 14tr, 15br, 16tr, 17, 18cl, 19r, 21–23, 24b, 25, 26b, 27tl, 27b, 28tr, 30r, 31l, 32r, 33t, 34l, 35l, 35bl, 36r, 39l, 40, 41, 42t, 43, 46tl, 46b, 48t, 49tl, 52b, 53tl, 54c, 56r, 56bl, 58, 60l, 60cr, 61, 62r, 63br, 64l, 68tl, 69b, 70r, 72tr, 76r, 87t, 92c, 92r, 94, 98tr, 101l, 102l, 102t, 102r, 103t, 103bc, 103br, 104bc, 104br, 106, 107tr, 107bl, 107br, 108tr, 110–114, 116b, 116tl, 117l, 119, 120, 122tl, 122tc, 122br, 123, 130–131, 133l, 134l, 135, 136l, 141–143, 146bl, 146r, 147, 158, 159, 161, 165l, 166, 168, 169, 171l, 172l, 172bl, 173r, 174, 175t, 175bl, 184b, 185, 188b, 195, 199t.

© Coll. Bénichou: pp. 62l, 63tr.

© Coll. Charlot: p. 46tr.

© Coll. Kharbine Tapabor: p. 173l.

© Coll. Lucien Camus: p. 60bc.

© Coll. Robles: p. 47.

© Coll.Dr Cottenceau: p. 32l.

© D. Brauermann: pp. 128, 129.

© D.R.: p. 14br.

© Daniel Fallot/I.N.A.: pp. 196, 197.

© Daniel Walland/Top Foto/Roger Viollet: p. 89.

© Dobrenn: pp. 38tl, 39c.

© Editingserver.com/L'Express: p. 164.

© Éditions Grasset: p. 28br.

© G.L. Manuel/Éditions Grasset: p. 28br.

© George Henri: p. 124.

© Getty Images: p. 4.

© Henri Cartier-Bresson/Magnum: pp. 68r, 82–84.

© Henri Martinie/Roger Viollet: p. 137r.

© Henriette Grindat: p. 144.

© Hulton-Deutsch/Corbis: pp. 134r, 155.

© I.N.A.: p. 18br.

© Jacques Ferrandez/Gallimard: p. 174.

© Jean Bernard/Aix-en-Provence: pp. 20tr, 26c, 34tr, 48tr, 48b, 50, 51tl, 52t, 53tr, 64r, 65l, 68bl, 72cr, 73, 122tr, 142bc, 142br, 151b, 173l, 198r.

© Keystone/Eyedea Presse: p. 19tl.

© Keystone-France/Keystone/Eyedea Presse: p. 171br.

© Kurt Hutton/Getty Images: p. 153.

© Lecordier Julien/Hoa-qui/Eyedea Illustration: p. 201.

© Leonno Jean/Life Pictures: pp. 172, 175br.

© Loomis Dean/Time Life Pictures/Getty Images: pp. 167, 171t, 178r, 181l.

© M. Jarnoux Coll. Oettly: p. 76l.

© ParisMatch/Potier: p. 186.

© Parry Roger/Ministère de la Culture – Médiathèque du Patrimoine, Dist-RMN: p. 31r.

© Popper foto/Getty Images: p. 192.

© René Dazy/Rue des Archives: p. 31br.

© René Saint Paul/Rue des Archives: pp. 29, 65r, 69t, 71, 72tl, 72bl, 72bc, 79tr, 79bl, 85, 108bl, 109r, 121bl, 127l, 182t.

© René Saint Paul: pp. 70, 108bl, 133r.

© Reportage-bild, Stockholm: pp. 188t, 189, 190t, 191t.

© Roger Carlet: p. 77t.

© Roger Viollet/Charles Hurault: p. 14l.

© Roger Viollet: pp. 10tr, 11r, 12b, 15, 16tl, 16b, 18t, 35tr, 59l, 60tr, 63l, 88, 104tr, 106b, 140r, 142tr, 145, 162t, 169, 181r, 190b, 200r.

© Rue des Archives/AGIP: pp. 39r, 74b, 77b, 79tl, 79br, 132l, 184, 191b.

© Rue des Archives/BCA/CSV: p. 88b

© Rue des Archives/BCA: pp. 66, 100.

© Rue des Archives/FIA: p. 78.

© Rue des Archives/RDA: pp. 27tl, 30l, 79t, 107tl

© Rue des Archives/Tal/Dobrenn: pp. 5t, 8, 56bc.

© Rue des Archives/Tal: pp. 5cl, 10br, 18bl, 59r, 74l, 90l, 91tc, 95, 102bc, 103bl, 104l, 105, 121tr, 202.

© Seeberger Frères/Rue des Archives: p. 72b.

© Selva/Gallimard: p. 20t.

© Studio Lipnitzki/Roger Viollet: pp. 78tr, 115l, 116tr, 117r, 118, 122bl, 125, 137l, 194.

© Süddeutsche Zeitung/Rue des Archives: pp. 56tl, 75b.

© Swim Ink 2, LLC/Corbis: p. 24t.

© Terreni: p. 180.

© Thurber/Gallimard: pp. 154, 155b.

© Ullstein Bild/Roger Viollet: pp. 5b, 138.

© US National Archives/Roger Viollet: p. 101tr.

© Viton: p. 38bl.

© Walt Disney: pp. 156, 157.

Cover: © Aisa/Roger Viollet

Images on the flaps:
© Bernand/CDDS Bernand

We made our best effort to find all holders of rights. If this was not possible for one or the other image, we would request the holder of rights to contact us.

Editorial Director

Aurèle Cariès

Artistic Director

Chloé Madeline

Image processing: Turquoise – Émerainville (77)